WEST AFRICA

Travel Guide 2025

Walk with Confidence: Throughout the region.

By

Johan Mia

Disclaimer

Dear Shopper,

I appreciate you for looking over this West Africa travel guide for your next vacation. In this guide, there are no pictures or maps. I've done my best to provide accurate and comprehensive information on West Africa. It's vital to remember that this book mainly focuses on literary descriptions, advice, and travel tips to enhance your holiday. You may make the most of your stay in West Africa by using the thoughts, advice, and information I have carefully chosen to share with you.

Please be aware that without visual aids like pictures and maps, you may need to rely on other sources for visual navigation or reference when visiting West Africa. I advise utilizing online resources like local maps or tourist information centers to supplement the material in this book.

The Purpose and Goals of This West Africa Travel Guide

This West Africa travel guide focuses on safety, cultural understanding, accessibility, and navigation. It provides essential safety insights and preparation strategies, covering security practices, local laws, customs, and emergency contacts. It emphasizes cultural respect and social etiquette, helping travelers navigate social interactions with confidence. The guide also offers practical advice on transportation options, navigation tips, and language essentials, ensuring readers can explore West Africa confidently and independently. This guide aligns with its subtitle, providing inspiration and practical knowledge for travelers.

TABLE OF CONTENT

CHAPTER ONE

Introduction to West Africa

West Africa is home to many vibrant cultures, stunning landscapes, and intriguing histories. It is a region that has been woven together from the threads of many different civilizations. West Africa spans from the Atlantic Ocean to the Sahel and from the Sahara Desert to the Gulf of Guinea. It is composed of 16 different countries, each of which has a unique history to contribute. In this article, we embark on an excursion to expose you to the fascinating world of West Africa, where tradition and modernity coexist and the spirit of innovation and resilience prevails.

Geographical Diversity and Landscapes

A geographical wonder is West Africa. The Sahara Desert's golden dunes in the north and lush tropical rainforests in the south make up its borders, which also include a startling variety of other landscapes. The area is fortunate to have powerful rivers like the Niger and Senegal, which have supported civilizations for ages. Its boundaries include huge savannas, lush hills, and picturesque coasts, all of which add to the region's rich mosaic.

The Cultural Tapestry of West Africa

One of the most unique features of West Africa is the diversity of its cultures. It has a long history of incorporating a wide range of languages, religions, and ethnic groups. Among the ethnic groups depicted in the millennium-long cultural tapestry are the Fulani of Mali, the Ashanti of Ghana, the Yoruba of Nigeria, and the Mandinka of The Gambia. Each group contributes its unique customs, dances, music, and cuisine, creating a colorful kaleidoscope of experiences. West Africa's artistic achievements are just amazing. The region is renowned for its vibrant textiles, exquisite beadwork, and exquisite wood sculptures. The bronze and terracotta sculptures from ancient countries like Ife and Benin continue to captivate art enthusiasts worldwide.

The rhythmic beating of traditional drums, the lyrical kora and balafon music, and the lively galleries of cities like Lagos and Dakar are blooming with contemporary African art, captivating both locals and visitors. Empires, trade routes, and cross-cultural exchanges are the threads that weave together West Africa's history. Scholars and businessmen from distant lands were drawn to ancient kingdoms such as Ghana, Mali, and Songhai because they were centers of wealth and knowledge.

The trans-Saharan trade routes connected West Africa to the Arab world, bringing with them goods, ideas, and religions such as Islam. The historical background of the area continues to shape its architecture, language, and religious customs. Despite its vast cultural and historical legacy, West Africa faces several challenges. Poverty, political instability, and health problems have presented major obstacles to advancement. However, the people's perseverance is evident. West Africans still respect their traditions, adapt to modern society, and work together to overcome obstacles. Initiatives in education, healthcare, and entrepreneurship are changing the landscape and promising a better future.

Just waiting to be explored, West Africa is a captivating continent rich in resilience, diversity, and inventiveness. Its vast landscapes, thriving civilizations, and legendary history will make it a treasure trove for both scholars and adventurers. As we go deeper into this fascinating region in future postings, we will uncover the little-known secrets and undiscovered treasures that make West Africa such a great place. Thus, return often for more explorations of the rich cultural diversity of West Africa.

Tips for Exploring West Africa

Take into account these suggestions to make the most of your trip in this diverse area:

Research and Plan: Prioritize your research on the nations you intend to visit. Schedule your travels in accordance with each destination's distinct attractions and necessities.

Visa and Documentation: Check the necessary paperwork and visa requirements well in advance. While some nations give visas on arrival, others can need applicants to submit applications in advance.

Health Precautions: Consult a travel clinic for information on immunisations and health precautions. Take anti-malarial medication and bring mosquito repellent because malaria is common in several West African nations.

Local Cuisine: Enjoy the regional cuisine, but exercise caution while eating street food. To reduce the danger of foodborne infections, select well-known booths and eateries.

Respect Local Customs: The varied civilizations of West Africa each have their own traditions and customs. To demonstrate respect, dress modestly and become familiar with regional customs.

Transportation: Expect a wide range of transit alternatives, including contemporary buses, shared taxis and daring bush cabs. Be ready for lengthy, rough rides.

Language: To improve communication, learn some fundamental French, English, or regional dialects.

Safety: Be on the lookout for potential dangers and stay alert, especially in busy places. Keep important documents safe, and be wary of con artists.

Currency: Keep local cash on hand because access to ATMs may be restricted in some areas.

Embrace the Adventure: From trekking through jungles to discovering historic sites like Timbuktu, West Africa provides one-of-a-kind experiences. Accept the challenge, interact with the populace, and enjoy the lively culture of the area.

Historical Significance

West Africa's long and varied history is incredibly significant historically. Following are some significant events in West African history:

Ancient Civilizations: The Ghana Empire, the Mali Empire, and the Songhai Empire were only a few of the numerous strong and significant ancient civilizations that inhabited West Africa. These dynasties presided over huge swaths of land, promoted trade, and helped Islam take root in the area. The Mali country in particular was famed for its wealth and Mansa Musa, its most well-known monarch, who traveled to Mecca on a well-known pilgrimage to display the prosperity of the country.

Trans-Saharan Trade: West Africa played a key role as a crossroads in the trans-Saharan trade routes that linked the interior of Africa to North Africa and the Mediterranean. During the medieval era, trade in goods like gold, salt, ivory, and other materials was crucial to the development of the world economy and the exchange of cultures.

Islam's spread: The introduction of Islam to West Africa resulted in profound changes for the region. Islam became the official religion of the empires of Ghana, Mali, and Songhai, which stimulated the development of Islamic thought, architecture, and Arabic writing systems.

Atlantic Slave Trade: West Africa played a tragically important role in the Atlantic Slave Trade. Millions of Africans were forcibly brought to the Americas as slaves while European powers built forts and trading stations along the coast. The African diaspora is still impacted by the effects of this tragic period in history.

Colonialism: In the late 19th century, West African countries were colonized by European colonial powers such as Britain, France, and Portugal. The region's political and social systems saw substantial changes throughout this time, and its resources were also exploited.

Independence Movements: The decolonization effort was greatly aided by West African countries including Ghana, Nigeria, and Senegal. African leaders like Kwame Nkrumah and Nnamdi Azikiwe pushed for independence and the creation of independent republics in the continent. In 1957, Ghana became the first country in sub-Saharan Africa to declare independence from colonial authority, paving the way for other countries to do the same.

Cultural Contributions: West Africa offers a broad range of musical traditions, colorful visual arts, elaborate weaving traditions, and storytelling customs. These cultural components still have an impact on culture both locally and globally.

Modern Challenges: West Africa currently faces a number of difficulties, such as political unrest, extreme poverty, deteriorating health conditions, and environmental problems. However, its resilient past, cultural diversity, and historical accomplishments continue to be significant indicators of its historical importance. Family, West Africa's ancient civilizations, role in trans-Saharan trade, expansion of Islam, engagement in the Atlantic Slave Trade, struggles for freedom, and its lively cultural contributions are what make it significant historically and have a long-lasting effect on the world.

Discovering the Richness of West African

West Africa is a diverse region with a rich cultural heritage and breathtaking landscapes that extend well beyond its borders. Nestled along the Atlantic coast, this region is renowned for its diverse landscapes, which range from the harsh Sahara Desert in Mali and Niger to the lush rainforests of countries like Ghana and Nigeria. West Africa is a treasure trove of culture. It was the birthplace of several significant empires, including the Songhai Empire and the enduring Mali Empire. The enduring influence of Islam, the rich oral traditions, and the stunning architecture of Timbuktu all attest to the legacy of these empires. West Africa's rich musical heritage cannot be discussed without complimenting it. The region's resonant kora and djembe rhythms influenced two international music genres: jazz and blues. Due to the modernization of indigenous rhythms by artists such as Fela Kuti, Afrobeats has become a worldwide sensation.

A vast array of delicious dishes may also be found in West Africa. From waakye to jollof rice, the cuisine is a delectable blend of flavors and ingredients that represent the region's many ethnic communities. The bustling marketplaces, including Kumasi's Kejetia Market, provide crafts, fabrics, and spices. Essentially, the riches of West Africa is more than just material belongings; it is a wealth of experiences, history, and culture that captivate and motivate people worldwide.

Rich Traditions and Ethnic Diversity

A fabric created by centuries of history, culture, and migration, West Africa is renowned for its illustrious traditions and astounding ethnic diversity. This huge area of land is home to numerous nations, including Senegal, Mali, Ghana, Nigeria, and many more. Each of these nations adds a distinct element to the vibrant tapestry that is West African culture.

Its wide variety of ethnic groups—which number in the hundreds—is one of West Africa's most alluring features. Each group brings its own languages, customs, and forms of expression to the table, including the Yoruba and Igbo of Nigeria, the Ashanti of Ghana, and the Fulani of Mali. From food to clothes, music, and dance, these ethnic identities are intricately woven into day-to-day existence.

Traditional practices in West Africa frequently have strong spiritual underpinnings. Despite the fact that many populations follow modern religions or adhere to traditional ones like Islam and Christianity, animist practices and beliefs nevertheless have an impact on modern society. Traditional ceremonies are lively displays of cultural heritage and spirituality, such as the Durbar celebration in Nigeria or the Homowo festival in Ghana

A highlight of the area is its diverse gastronomic offerings, which include , fufu, and jollof rice, which attract food lovers from all over the world. With genres like Afrobeat and Highlife rising in popularity around the world, the sounds of West Africa are also enthralling. A testimonial to the continued vitality of West Africa's cultures is provided by the region's varied traditions and ethnic variety. This area's unique fusion of history, spirituality, and creativity continues to attract and inspire people all over the world, making West Africa a veritable treasure trove of cultural treasures.

CHAPTER TWO

Languages and Communication

The incredible diversity of West African languages and communication reflects the region's complex fabric of cultures and traditions. West Africa is one of the most varied regions in the world, with over 1,000 different languages spoken there. The Niger-Congo, Afroasiatic, and Nilo-Saharan language families, among others, can be generally divided into which these languages belong.

The Niger-Congo language: family, which includes Hausa, Yoruba, Igbo, and Swahili, is the biggest in West Africa. Languages of the Niger-Congo region are well recognised for their wide use of tonal differences, in which a word's pitch or tone can alter its meaning. They frequently have strong oral traditions, with proverbs and storytelling being important tools for communication.

Afroasiatic Languages: Arabic is a member of the Afroasiatic language family and is mainly used in the Sahel region of West Africa. In especially among Muslim communities, Arabic is employed for religious, educational, and governmental purposes.

Nilo-Saharan languages: which include languages like Kanuri and Songhai, are primarily spoken in the northeastern region of West Africa. These languages are renowned for having intricate grammatical structures and are frequently connected to pastoralist and nomadic cultures. West African languages allow for non-verbal communication as well. It frequently combines verbal and non-verbal cues, including body language, facial emotions, and gestures. In addition, oral storytelling has a long history in many West African civilizations, where stories, history, and cultural values are transmitted from one generation to the next.

English, French, and Portuguese are now more frequently used in government and corporate communication in West Africa as a result of the continent's increased urbanization and globalization. Local languages are still essential for conserving cultural history and facilitating intercommunity contact. Furthermore, the development of West African communication is being influenced by technology and the internet.

People are able to connect in their original languages and share their cultures with a worldwide audience thanks to social media, mobile apps, and internet platforms. The region's cultural diversity and richness are vividly reflected in the languages and communication of West Africa. While maintaining the distinct identities of the speakers, these languages are still evolving and adapting to the dynamics of the modern world.

Commonly Spoken Languages

The people of West Africa speak a wide variety of languages, making the area linguistically diverse. Although West Africa is home to hundreds of different languages, only a select few are more frequently understood and spoken. The following are some of the languages that are widely used in West Africa: One of the most extensively spoken languages in West Africa is Hausa, which is mostly spoken in Nigeria, Niger, as well as in some areas of Ghana, Sudan, and Cameroon. It facilitates contact between many ethnic groups and is the common language of Northern Nigeria.

Yoruba: Benin, Togo, and southwest Nigeria are the main speaking areas for this language. It is well-known for its dynamic literary and artistic forms and has a rich cultural and historical value.

Igbo: Igbo has a vast population of speakers and is mainly spoken in southeast Nigeria.

It has distinctive language characteristics and is important to the Igbo people's culture.

Fulfulde (Fula): The Fula or Fulani people live in nations including Senegal, Mali, Niger, and Nigeria and speak Fulfulde. It's a dialect-rich nomadic language.

Wolof: Wolof is a language spoken in Senegal and the Gambia. It has a rich oral heritage that includes proverbs and storytelling. Additionally, Senegal's official language is this one.

Mandingo (Bambara): Also referred to as Bambara, the Mandingo language is used in Mali, Guinea, and a few locations in Senegal and the Gambia. It has a key role in both West African music and literature.

Twi: Twi is a significant Akan tongue used in Ghana. It has a rich cultural legacy and is the language that is most often used in the Ashanti region.

Pular (Peul): Pular, often referred to as Fula, is a West African language that is spoken in countries including Guinea, Senegal, Mali, and Niger. Nomadic pastoralists utilize it frequently.

Mende: The southern and eastern parts of Sierra Leone, in particular, are home to the Mende language. The Mende people speak it and employ a number of dialects.

These are only a few instances of the languages that are widely used throughout West Africa. Each language in the area has its own distinct history and traditions, reflecting the region's rich cultural tapestry.

Learning Local Phrases and Greetings

Here are some regional greetings and expressions from West Africa:

Sannu da ki (Hausa) - In Hausa, this phrase is equivalent to "Hello, how's work?"

Akwaaba (Akan) - A customary salutation in Ghana that translates to "Welcome!"

Igbo's Nnoo is a straightforward salutation that sounds a lot like "Hello."

Barka da (Hausa) - It signifies "Welcome!" and is used to greet someone.

Sawubona This greeting in Zulu, which is largely spoken in Southern Africa, means "Hello" or "I see you."

I ni ce (Hausa) - This is Hausa for "What's your name?"

Mbote (Lingala) This greeting, which is used in places like the Congo, means "Hello."
"Kedu ka i mere?" (Igbo) - The "How are you?" The question is asked using the Igbo language.

Salam aleykum (Fulfulde) is a well-known salutation that translates to "Peace be upon you."

Nnoo o is an additional friendly Igbo greeting that is comparable to saying "Hello."

Aane (Wolof) is a colloquial greeting that is used in Senegal. The phrase "How are you doing?" has a similar meaning in Jamaican patois.

"**Na** " (Hausa) translates to "Thank you" in Hausa.

Kwasiada (Akan) is the phrase used to welcome someone in Ghana on a Sunday and means "Sunday welcome."

Sannu da is a formal Hausa greeting that means "Hello and welcome."

This Zulu greeting is used to say "Hello" to a gathering of people and is called "Sanibonani" in English.

The greetings may differ by location and community because West Africa is home to a wide variety of languages and cultures

Languages and Communication Etiquette

The linguistic and cultural diversity of West Africa is reflected in the region's diverse and rich communication and language traditions. West Africa is home to many different ethnic groups, each with its own languages and ways of communicating. Some crucial language and social conventions for this region are as follows:

Multilingualism: The linguistic variety in West Africa is well-known. People in this area frequently speak many languages. Although indigenous languages are frequently spoken, depending on the nation's history, many West Africans also speak colonial languages like English, French, or Portuguese.

Respect for Elders: In traditional West African civilizations, elder respect is highly valued. Younger people frequently employ respectful gestures and formal forms of speech when talking.

This may entail bowing, using particular pronouns, or addressing elders in a dignified manner.

Greetings: In West African communication etiquette, greetings are a crucial component. Many cultures regularly engage in handshakes, hugs, and other types of physical contact. Before starting the main discourse, verbal pleasantries are frequently complex and can include enquiring about the other person's family and general well-being.

Nonverbal Communication: Nonverbal cues, such as body language, eye contact, and facial expressions, are important in communication. While keeping eye contact can convey confidence and respect, it's important to avoid staring, as this can come across as rude.

Use of Proverbs and Stories: In West African communication, proverbs and storytelling are frequently used. Conversations become more interesting and meaningful when proverbs are utilized to impart knowledge and lessons.

Gift-Giving: In West African communities, giving and receiving presents is a popular custom, particularly while visiting someone's house or as a show of goodwill. It's crucial to observe regional gift-giving traditions.

Language as Identity: In West Africa, language and cultural identity are strongly related. Languages are a source of pride for many ethnic groups, who use them to protect their history. Building rapport can be greatly aided by learning a few simple words and phrases in the native tongue.

Religion's Influence: Islam and Christianity are two major religions in West African nations. It can have an impact on greetings and communication conventions, with Muslims frequently using the phrase "As-salamu alaykum" (peace be upon you).

Regional Variations: The many nations that make up West Africa each have their own unique cultural and linguistic quirks. When talking in the area, it's crucial to be aware of these regional variations.

Adaptability: People from West Africa are renowned for their friendliness and hospitality. Visitors are advised to be flexible and open-minded when conversing with locals because they may be understanding of cultural differences and value an honest attempt to do so. In conclusion, the varied cultures and traditions of West Africa are firmly ingrained in the languages and communication customs there. Successful relationships in this thriving and diverse region depend on having respect, being courteous, and having a basic awareness of local traditions.

Overcoming Language Barriers

West Africa has a complex linguistic landscape, making it challenging to overcome language hurdles. Here are some methods for overcoming these obstacles:

Learn Important Phrases: Begin by learning the fundamental words and phrases in the local tongues of the area you are in. In order to build rapport, simple greetings and polite sentiments can be very effective.

Employ Multilingual personnel: Having personnel who can speak various languages is invaluable if you're a member of an organization or team. Make use of their language abilities to promote communication.

Use Visual Aids: Since images, diagrams, and maps are easily comprehended by all people, they are effective instruments for communicating ideas to people of all languages.

Use online translation tools or download translation applications to assist with simultaneous language interpretation. These can be very helpful for last-minute communication requirements.

Hire local interpreters to help with language translation during meetings, negotiations, or other crucial encounters if at all possible.

Cultural Intelligence: Recognise the subtleties of the local culture. Being culturally sensitive can lessen miscommunications brought on by linguistic disparities.

Language Instruction: If your team members or employees deal with folks from West Africa frequently, consider investing in language instruction for them. Learning the native tongue demonstrates respect and dedication. Identify and employ common languages that are commonly spoken in the area, such as English, French, or Portuguese, as a means of communication as necessary.

Simplify Your Language: Speak slowly and in straightforward terms, avoiding colloquial idioms and difficult-to-translate vocabulary.

Non-Verbal Communication: When words are insufficient, pay close attention to non-verbal indicators like body language and gestures.

Empathy and Patience: When overcoming linguistic hurdles, exercise patience and understanding. Be understanding of those who might find it difficult to communicate in a foreign language.

Feedback Mechanisms: Create effective channels for people to express their opinions and ask questions if they don't grasp anything.

Develop linguistic diversity plans that include language instruction, interpreter services, and cultural awareness initiatives if you represent an organization working in West Africa.

Engage with the neighborhood to better understand the people there and their language and culture. This can promote harmony and enhance communication.

Investigate the use of technology, such as language applications or remote interpretation services, to promote communication in a variety of linguistic contexts.

It's important to keep in mind that overcoming language obstacles in West Africa, or any other location, is a continuous process that necessitates adaptability and flexibility to the region's linguistic and cultural variety.

Interactions and partnerships can succeed more when effective communication bridges are built.

CHAPTER THREE

Planning Your Trip To West African Trip

1. **Choose Your Destination:** West Africa is a diverse region with many countries to explore. Decide which countries you want to visit. Popular destinations include Nigeria, Ghana, Senegal, Ivory Coast, and Mali.

2. **Research and Documentation:** Check the entry requirements for each country you plan to visit. This includes visa requirements, vaccinations, and passport validity. Ensure all your travel documents are in order.

3. **Set a Budget:** Determine your travel budget, including accommodation, transportation, food, and activities. Consider currency exchange rates in your budgeting.

4. **Decide on Travel Dates:** Choose your travel dates and consider the best time to visit. West

Africa has a tropical climate, so weather can influence your experience.

5. **Book Flights:** Search for and book your flights to and from West Africa. Try to find the best deals, and consider open-jaw flights if you plan to visit multiple countries.

6. **Accommodation**: Research and book accommodation in advance. Options range from hotels to guesthouses and Airbnb. Ensure they meet your budget and safety standards.

7. **Health Preparations:** Consult a travel clinic for vaccinations and health advice. Carry essential medications and a first-aid kit.

8. **Travel Insurance:** Purchase comprehensive travel insurance that covers medical emergencies, trip cancellations, and other unexpected events.

9. **Create an Itinerary:** Plan your daily activities, including visits to attractions, tours, and relaxation time. Be flexible and open to changes.

10. **Packing**: Pack light but include appropriate clothing for the climate, as well as essentials like

power adapters, insect repellent, and a good travel guidebook.

11. **Money Matters:** Inform your bank of your travel plans to avoid issues with your cards. Carry some local currency and a backup card in case of emergencies.

12. **Language and Culture:** Learn some basic phrases in the local languages and read about the culture and customs of the region you're visiting.

13. **Safety Precautions:** Research safety tips for the specific countries you're visiting and stay informed about any travel advisories.

14. **Transportation Within the Region:** Plan how you'll get around within West Africa. Options include domestic flights, buses, and shared taxis.

15. **Stay Connected:** Purchase a local SIM card for your phone to stay connected and consider downloading offline maps and translation apps.

16. **Respect Local Customs:** Be respectful of local customs, traditions, and dress codes. This will help you have a more enjoyable and culturally immersive experience.

17. **Stay Healthy:** Eat at reputable restaurants, drink bottled water, and practice good hygiene to minimize the risk of foodborne illnesses.

18. **Emergency Contacts:** Keep a list of emergency contacts, including your country's embassy or consulate in the region.

19. **Enjoy Your Trip:** Finally, embrace the adventure, make new friends, and savor the unique experiences that West Africa has to offer.

Choosing the Best Time to Visit

The country you intend to visit, as well as your preferences for weather and activities, will determine when is the ideal time to go to West Africa. West Africa experiences distinct wet and dry seasons due to its tropical environment. Here is a general rule of thumb: In general, the dry season, which lasts from November to March, is the ideal time to go to several West African nations, including Ghana, Senegal, and Nigeria. Less rain and a cooler climate make it perfect for outdoor activities and sightseeing.

Travel can be more difficult during the rainy season (April to October), which can deliver lush scenery and colorful foliage but can also make it more difficult because of the heavy rains and humidity. Road closures and flooding are possible in certain places. Saharan Region (e.g., Mali, Niger): To escape intense heat, it's better to travel to West Africa's desert regions like the Sahel during the milder months of November to February.

Visa Requirements and Travel Documentation

There are certain common considerations for travelers wishing to visit West African countries, while visa procedures and travel documentation may differ from one country in the region to another. Please be aware that the standards listed below may change anytime. I wrote this based on my knowledge as of April 2024. The most recent information must be confirmed with the relevant embassies or consulates before departure. Following are some general principles:

Passport: Make sure your passport is valid for at least six months after the day you plan to depart.

Make sure you have enough empty visa pages for stamps at the entrance and exit.

Visa prerequisites: Foreigners must obtain visas to enter the majority of West African nations. Check the exact criteria for your location as visa requirements can change.

For some nationalities, some countries provide visa-on-arrival options, however this also varies by nation.

Types of Visas: Tourist visas: are required for those who are going to West African nations for vacation, business, or family purposes.

Business Visa: If you intend to conduct business operations in the area, a business visa may be required. If you have a layover or intend to go via a West African nation in transit, you must obtain a transit visa.

Visa Request: The usual requirements are a visa application form, a current passport, two passport-sized pictures, and the necessary visa cost.

There can be a need for further paperwork, like a letter of invitation, proof of lodging, or a return ticket.

Requirements for immunisations: Prior to admission, several West African nations may demand confirmation of vaccines, such as yellow fever. Check the destination's unique vaccination needs.

Money and Charges: Depending on the nation, be ready to pay visa fees in either the local currency or in U.S. dollars.

Make sure you have enough local currency on hand or a mechanism to do so once you get there.

Norms for Entry and Exit: Keep duplicates of your passport, visa, and other important papers. Upon arrival, you might need to register with the local authorities in some countries.

Travel Protection: It is important to get complete travel insurance that includes trip cancellation and medical emergency coverage.

Health and Security Precautions: Keep abreast on local security developments and travel warnings. Observe any COVID-19 limits or health regulations that may be in effect.

Language: Although English and French are extensively spoken in many West African nations, it still helps to be familiar with some common local slang. Always check the official website of the embassy or consulate of the country you intend to visit for the most up-to-date and accurate information before your trip, keeping in mind that visa requirements and travel papers can change. For help with the visa application procedure, you may also want to speak with a travel agency or expert.

Health and Safety Precautions

Depending on the region and circumstance, health and safety precautions may vary in West Africa, but the following are some broad principles:

Equipment for personal protection (PPE): Wear the proper PPE, as necessary for your particular profession or occupation, including helmets, gloves, safety glasses, and high-visibility clothes. Make sure PPE is maintained properly and replaced when it is damaged.

Workplace Security: To reduce tripping hazards, keep work sites neat and organized. To identify dangerous situations or circumstances, use warning signs and barriers. Make sure that indoor work spaces have adequate ventilation and temperature control.

Fire Prevention: Install and keep fire extinguishers in places that are easily accessible. Regularly practice fire drills and make sure all employees are aware of escape routes.

Electricity Security: Regularly check and maintain your electrical equipment.Use grounded electrical outlets, to keep circuits from being overloaded. Employees should receive electrical safety training.

Chemical Security: Provide Material Safety Data Sheets (MSDS) for all hazardous substances and label and store chemicals properly. Workers should receive training on the proper handling and disposal of chemicals.

Machine Security: Make sure that equipment is properly maintained and guarded. Teach employees how to operate machinery and equipment safely.

Emergency Action: Create an emergency response strategy and inform every employee of it. Make sure staff members are trained in basic first aid and provide first aid equipment.

Controlling infectious diseases: Encourage healthy hygiene habits, such as consistent handwashing. Access to sanitary facilities and clean water should be available. Keep up with regional illness outbreaks and abide by public health regulations.

Safety Education: All personnel should get regular orientation and safety training. Give non-English speakers training materials that are relevant for their language.

Environment-Related Issues: Recognise and abide by any environmental laws in your community.
Recycle waste items when you can, and dispose of it responsibly.

Cultural Awareness: When putting safety measures into place, be mindful of regional customs and traditions.
Make sure the training materials and safety guidelines are acceptable for the local culture.

Community Participation: Engage the neighborhood to address safety issues and establish a good rapport.

Please keep in mind that these are merely basic recommendations, and it is essential to modify them in accordance with the unique conditions and laws of the West African region as well as the king of the work being done. For specific guidelines and laws in your location, you should consult local authorities and safety specialists.

Budgeting and Currency Exchange

West Africa's economic and financial environment depends heavily on budgeting and currency exchange. West Africa is a diversified region made up of 15 nations with various currencies and distinctive budgetary practices. We'll go through budgeting and currency conversion in West Africa in this section:

Currency Environment:

The West African CFA franc (XOF), which is backed by the French Treasury, is the common currency among the eight West African nations that make up the West African Economic and Monetary Union (WAEMU). These nations include Mali, Niger, Senegal, Togo, Guinea-Bissau, Ivory Coast, Burkina Faso, and Senegal. The Nigerian Naira (NGN) is the official currency of Nigeria, the most populous nation in West Africa. Other West African nations with their own national currencies include Ghana, Sierra Leone, Liberia, and the Gambia.

West African financial planning: Although each West African nation has its unique budgeting procedure and schedule, they all adhere to some of the same basic concepts. Annual budgets are often produced by regional governments, including the region's revenue streams, spending plans, and development priorities. Key industries like healthcare, education, infrastructure, agriculture, and social welfare are frequently covered by budgets. Some West African nations struggle to maintain fiscal discipline, which results in deficits and excessive debt levels.

International agencies like the World Bank and the International Monetary Fund (IMF) frequently collaborate with these nations to offer financial support and encourage budgetary discipline.

Currency Trade & Exchange: The exchange of currencies is necessary for commerce and economic interactions with regional and international partners. The West African CFA franc, which is the currency used by WAEMU nations, has a fixed exchange rate with the Euro, ensuring commercial stability. Cross-border trade and investment can be impacted by changes in the exchange rates between different national currencies.

Through projects like the West African Economic and Monetary Union (WAEMU) and the Economic Community of West African States (ECOWAS), the West African area is aiming towards deeper economic integration. Trade, investment, and currency stability are the objectives of these initiatives.

Obstacles and Possibilities:

For businesses and individuals in West Africa, devaluation of the local currency, inflation, and exchange rate fluctuation might present difficulties. In the area, there are opportunities for economic growth, notably in industries like agriculture, natural resources, and technology. In order to address shared difficulties, harmonize policies, and advance economic development, regional cooperation and integration activities are still ongoing.

In conclusion, currency exchange and budgeting are crucial to the economic growth of West African nations. The region's wide range of currencies and distinctive budgeting procedures reflect its incredibly diversified cultural and economic background. While obstacles still exist, regional projects and cooperative efforts seek to give West Africa's economy a more secure and prosperous future.

Health and Vaccination Recommendations

I can provide you some basic health and vaccine advice for West Africa, but it's crucial to speak with a healthcare provider or a travel clinic for specific suggestions catered to your itinerary and health situation. Please consult your healthcare practitioner for the most recent information as health hazards may vary throughout West African nations. Here are some suggestions for everyone:

Standard vaccinations: Make sure you are up to date on routine immunisations such the MMR, DTaP, and MMR (measles, mumps, rubella).

Vaccination against yellow fever: Entry into numerous West African nations frequently requires proof of inoculation against yellow fever. Get the vaccination at least 10 days before your trip and check the country's unique admission regulations.

Prevention of malaria: In many West African nations, malaria is a serious health danger. To find the right antimalarial drug, speak with your doctor.

Wear long sleeves and pants, apply insect repellent and sleep with a mosquito net to lower your chance of contracting diseases carried by mosquitoes.

Vaccinations for typhoid and hepatitis A: Typhoid and hepatitis A immunisations should be taken into consideration as these diseases can spread through tainted food and water.

Hepatitis B and cholera: You might also want to talk with your doctor about cholera and hepatitis B vaccinations, depending on your travel intentions and destinations.

Polio: Polio still exists in some West African nations. Make sure your polio immunisations are current.

Diarrhea from Travel: To prevent getting traveler's diarrhea, be cautious with your food and beverage intake. Avoid eating raw or undercooked food, and stick to bottled or purified water.

Travel Protection: Think about getting travel insurance that includes evacuation in the event of a serious illness or injury and medical emergency.

Medications on prescription: Bring enough of your medications and a prescription in case you need a refill if you have any chronic medical issues.

Warnings for your health: Maintain proper hygiene by regularly washing your hands with soap and water. Make sure that the food is prepared and served in sanitary circumstances when eating street food. Have a strategy in place for emergency medical care and be aware of the nearby healthcare services. It's important to be informed and speak with a healthcare provider for the most recent advice before your journey to West Africa because health recommendations can change over time.

Currency and Banking Information

West Africa's banking and currency information is broad and complex because it includes the financial systems of numerous nations in the region. West Africa is home to a number of nations, each of which has its own currency. The Nigerian Naira (NGN) and the West African CFA franc (XOF) are two of the more well-known currencies. Eight nations in West Africa that are a part of the West African Economic and Monetary Union (WAEMU) all utilize the West African CFA franc. These nations include Mali, Niger, Senegal, Togo, Guinea-Bissau, Ivory Coast, Burkina Faso, and Senegal. The Naira is the national currency of Nigeria, one of the largest economies in the region.

Banking Systems: The sophistication and regulatory structures of the banking systems in West Africa differ. The region's major cities typically have well-established national and international banking infrastructure. Important financial hubs include Abidjan in Ivory Coast and Lagos in Nigeria.

Central banks: The monetary policy and regulation are the responsibility of the central banks in many West African nations. For instance, the Central Bank of Nigeria (CBN) controls the Naira, while the Central Bank of West African States (BCEAO) is in charge of the West African CFA franc. These central banks are essential for maintaining financial stability and currency stability.

Financial inclusion: In order to attract more people and companies to the formal banking system, efforts have been made to promote financial inclusion in West Africa. People in remote places can now more easily access banking services because of the growth of mobile banking and digital financial services.

West Africa's banking and currency systems encounter a number of difficulties. Concerns about currency depreciation, the need for more financial awareness, and initiatives to combat financial crimes including fraud and money laundering are a few of these.

Travel Kit and Packing Essentials

Your kit and other packing essentials for West Africa may vary depending on your specific travel itinerary and the countries you'll be visiting. The following is a list of considerations along with justifications for each: Verify that your passport will still be valid six months after the date you want to return. Before you go, confirm the country-specific visa requirements.

Invest in comprehensive travel insurance that covers medical emergencies, trip cancellation, and theft. Pack a compact medical kit with essentials like pain relievers, antimalarial drugs, and any prescribed prescriptions, and ask a travel doctor for advice on any necessary vaccinations. If you're visiting West Africa, bring an effective insect repellent that contains DEET because there's a significant risk of becoming malaria.

Sun protection: To shield yourself from the potent African sun, use sunscreen, sunglasses, and a wide-brimmed hat.

Travel adapter: Because multiple plug types may be present in West Africa, a universal travel adapter is useful. Pack breathable, light-weight clothing that is appropriate for the tropical environment. To avoid mosquitoes, think about wearing long sleeves and trousers.

Comfy Footwear: For strolling and casual outings, wear sturdy, comfy shoes. 1trip documents: Securely kept photocopies or digital copies of your passport, visa, trip insurance, and any other relevant papers.

Money and Cards: Inform your bank of your vacation plans and bring a combination of local currency in cash and credit/debit cards. In some places, access to ATMs may be restricted.

Water purification: To ensure that the water is safe to consume, a portable water filter or purification pills may be helpful.

Travel towel: A small, quickly drying towel is useful.

Toiletries: The bare necessities, including toilet paper as it may not always be accessible.

SIM card: Consider purchasing a local SIM card for inexpensive data and local calls.

Language Guide: For communication, a phrasebook or language-learning software for the regional tongues can be useful.

Maps and GPS: For navigation in rural locations, use offline maps or a GPS unit.

Locks: Use combination locks or cable locks during travel to safeguard your belongings.

Snacks: Carry some non-perishable snacks for times when food may be difficult to come by.

Photocopy: Share a photocopy of your travel schedule with a family member or acquaintance you can trust.

Earplugs and a travel pillow can help make long trips more comfortable.

Bring your camera and any necessary gear if you enjoy taking pictures.

Items that limit plastic waste include a reusable water bottle, utensils, and shopping bags.

Respectful Attire: Dress modestly when visiting places of worship or politically conservative neighborhoods.

Keep in mind that particular goods may change depending on your own needs and the nations you intend to visit. Prior to your journey, always do your homework and verify the most recent West African travel restrictions and advisories.

CHAPTER FOUR

Crossing Borders: Overland Adventures

A journey throughout West Africa by land is full of diverse topography, vibrant cultures, and the thrill of crossing borders that set this continent apart. This trip promises to be unique and enlightening for anyone wishing to travel to the interior of Africa.

Starting Point: The majority of overland trips in West Africa start in coastal towns like Lagos, Nigeria, or' Dakar, Senegal. These bustling metropolises offer a glimpse of modern African life before venturing into the hinterlands. There are many different cultures, languages, and customs throughout West Africa. Visitors can explore Ghana's colorful festivals, encounter the nomadic Tuareg people in the Sahara Desert, or meander through the bustling marketplaces of Bamako, Mali. Crossing a border reveals a new facet of culture to explore.

Scenic Wonders: Travelers experience a wide range of scenery while traveling overland. From the parched dunes of the Sahara Desert to the lush rainforests of Sierra Leone, West Africa's natural beauty is stunning. When crossing international borders, one often notices a dramatic change in the surroundings.

Animal Encounters: There are many different kinds of animals in West Africa, and visitors can view lions, elephants, and a vast variety of birds in national parks like Niokolo-Koba in Senegal and Pendjari in Benin. Crossing foreign borders adds to the intrigue of visiting these protected areas.

Culinary Delights: The cuisine has a big impact on the journey. Every country has its own unique culinary offerings. From thieboudienne in Senegal to jollof rice in Nigeria, overland travelers can savor a wide range of cuisines.

Community Involvement: Many overland adventurers use their time to engage with the locals by participating in customs or lending a hand with community initiatives. These discussions foster long-lasting relationships and deepen our knowledge of West African culture.

In West Africa, overland travel may be challenging and exciting. Unreliable infrastructure, challenging roads, and border crossings might try one's patience. However, these challenges also give the journey a sense of excitement. It's common to encounter hospitable locals along the way who provide advice or share stories. West Africa has a lengthy history that includes ties to ancient civilizations, colonial legacies, and the transatlantic slave trade. Entering historical sites that provide a comprehensive understanding of the region's past, like Goree Island in Senegal or Elmina Castle in Ghana, is often necessary while crossing borders.

In West Africa, cross-country overland trips combine history, culture, environment, and human interaction in an intriguing way. The opportunities they provide to visit this dynamic and diverse region are few and far between. The path may be challenging at times for those who dare to embark on this amazing journey, but the benefits are limitless, making it an experience that will never be forgotten.

Public Transportation Options

West Africa is a diversified region with a variety of public transit options. Following is a list and explanation of some popular modes of public transport in West Africa:

Buses: In several West African nations, buses are a common form of public transportation. They come in a variety of shapes and sizes, including big interstate buses, little minibosses, and shared taxis.

Buses are frequently a cheap means of getting around cities and urban regions. In West African cities and towns, taxis are common. There are several locations where shared taxis travel predetermined routes and pick up passengers along the way. In others, you can arrange a private cab ride.

Tro-Tros: Particularly popular in Ghana, tro-tros are a distinctive form of shared minibus transportation. They follow set itineraries and are distinguished by their vibrant artwork. Tro-Tros are a practical means of transportation in cities and towns.

Motorcycle Taxis (Okadas): Popular for short distances, motorcycle taxis—also referred to as Okadas—are a common kind of transportation. In crowded urban locations, they are frequently used to negotiate through heavy traffic. In Nigeria and some other West African nations, these three-wheeled keke (auto rickshaws) are frequently used for short journeys. They offer a more plush substitute for motorbike taxis.

Trains: Although West Africa's train infrastructure is less developed than that of some other continents, several nations, such Nigeria and Senegal, have railway networks that link their major cities. For longer journeys, trains can be a beautiful and cozy means of transportation.

Boats and Ferries: Given the number of rivers and beaches in West Africa, boats and ferries are an important mode of transportation. They are frequently employed to bridge rivers and get to coastal or island villages.

Metro systems: In a few West African cities, including Lagos (Nigeria) and Abidjan (Ivory Coast), there are metro systems that offer a practical way to travel around congested urban regions.

Domestic Flights: Many West African nations have airports with domestic flights tying up big cities for longer trips and international travel. This is the route that covers the area the quickest.

Renting a car is an alternative for those who value comfort and flexibility. Planning is necessary because traffic and road conditions might fluctuate greatly.

Renting Vehicles and Driving Tips

A valid driving license, your passport, and an international driving permit are among the documentation you should have. You should confirm the particular requirements for each West African nation you intend to visit.

Vehicle rental: Pick a dependable company. Before you leave, check the car's condition and make a note of any damage that may be there. Make sure you comprehend all of the rental conditions, including the insurance and fuel rules.

Traffic Regulations: Become familiar with the laws and restrictions that apply to local traffic. Countries may have different right-of-way laws, speed limits, and road signs.

Route Conditions: Be ready for a variety of conditions on the route, from paved highways to winding, uneven roads. A 4WD vehicle might be useful in rural locations where there may be unpaved roads. Make sure your car has the necessary safety features, such as seat belts, functional headlights, and indicators. Keep a first aid kit, fire extinguisher, and warning triangles on you at all times.

Navigation: Since certain regions may have inadequate signage, use GPS navigation or smartphone apps to assist with instructions. In the event of low connectivity, think about downloading offline maps.

Local Driving Customs: Take note of and adjust to local driving customs. Drivers can be aggressive in some West African nations, and traffic laws may not always be rigorously adhered to. Driving defensively is frequently important. Planning your gasoline stops is important because there might not be many petrol outlets in distant places. Bring extra water, snacks, and a small toolkit with you just in case. Having local currency on hand will help you pay for tolls, bribes (which, regrettably, can be a problem in some places), and other little purchases. In rural areas, credit cards can not be frequently accepted.

Language: Since English and French aren't always spoken in the area, it's a good idea to learn some basic local phrases or carry about a translation software.

Safety and Security: Pay attention to your surroundings and steer clear of nighttime driving, especially in rural areas. When stopped in traffic, keep the windows up and the doors locked.

Border crossings: Be aware of the rules for obtaining a visa and clearing customs when traveling between West African nations. Ensure that your car is properly documented, including any temporary import permissions necessary.

Contacts for the embassy and local emergency services should be saved in your phone. Have a contact at home who is aware of your itinerary as well.

Health Precautions: Be sure to bring a basic medical kit and to have any necessary vaccinations. To prevent disease, be mindful about the food and drink you consume.

Local aid: Keep the phone numbers of nearby mechanics, towing companies, and aid providers handy in case of emergencies or breakdowns. It's important to keep in mind that traveling in West Africa can be an exciting and culturally interesting experience, but it's also important to be prepared and flexible in case something unexpected happens.

Navigating Border Crossings and Customs

Crossing borders and navigating West African traditions may be both exciting and difficult. West Africa is made up of 16 different countries, each with its own unique language, culture, and customs. Below is a synopsis of what to expect when crossing borders in this region:

Documentation: Verify that your passport is valid for at least six months and that it is up to date. Since many West African countries require a visa for entry, find out and obtain the necessary visas in advance. Certain countries, including those that comprise the Economic Community of West African States (ECOWAS), allow their residents to travel with just their identification card.

Health Requirements: Some governments may need confirmation of vaccinations, especially for diseases like yellow fever.

Make sure to research the specific health criteria for each country you plan to visit and bring the required documentation. Be ready to declare any goods you are bringing into the country, including money, electronics, and other items. Since each nation has its own set of customs rules, it is essential to familiarize yourself with them in advance to avoid any issues.

Language Barrier: English, French, and Portuguese are the three most commonly spoken languages in West Africa. However, there are many regional languages. Learning a few basic words and phrases in the local language might be helpful, particularly when speaking with immigration and customs officials who may not speak English. When traveling across borders, exercise patience as wait times might vary significantly. At crowded border crossings, long lineups may form, although smaller ones may move faster. Try to arrive early to minimize traffic and be prepared for perhaps lengthy waits.

Bribery and Corruption: Unfortunately, corruption is an issue at some border crossings. Be cautious and try to abide by the guidelines. Keep any pertinent documentation handy, and avoid accepting bribes as this could lead to legal action.

Currency Exchange: To cover upfront expenses, it's a good idea to exchange some cash at the border as not all establishments accept credit cards. When using dubious money changers, use caution and ensure that you receive a reasonable rate. Before crossing borders, learn about the many transit options accessible. It can be challenging to find safe transportation because some borders are far distant. Hiring a local guide or driver could be beneficial.

Security: Find out how safe the place you plan to visit is. Some border areas may be vulnerable to violence or conflict, so remain alert and exercise caution when necessary.

Act locally to show respect for area customs and standards. Being courteous and friendly can make crossing borders much easier. Remember that crossing a border in West Africa can present unique challenges and experiences. By planning ahead, staying educated, and maintaining your flexibility, you can successfully navigate the challenges of crossing borders in this fascinating and varied region.

Documentation: Make sure your passport is current and has at least six months left on its validity. Research and secure the required visas in advance as admission into many West African nations requires a visa. Some nations, such as those that make up the Economic Community of West African States (ECOWAS), permit citizens of member states to travel with only an ID card.

Health Requirements: Particularly for diseases like yellow fever, certain governments may demand proof of vaccinations. For each nation you intend to visit, be sure to research the specific health requirements and bring the necessary papers. Be prepared to disclose any products you are bringing into the nation, such as cash, gadgets, and other stuff. Every country has its own set of customs laws, therefore it is crucial to research them beforehand to prevent any problems.

Language Barrier: In West Africa, the three most widely used languages are English, French, and Portuguese. There are numerous regional languages, though. It can be beneficial to learn a few fundamental words and phrases in the local tongue, especially when interacting with customs and immigration authorities who might not speak English. Be patient when crossing borders because wait periods can differ greatly. Long lines could form at busy border crossings, although smaller ones might move more quickly. To avoid traffic and be ready for potentially long waits, try to arrive early.

Bribery and Corruption: At some border crossings, corruption unfortunately presents a problem. Be careful, and make an effort to follow the rules. Keep any relevant paperwork close at hand, and refrain from paying bribes as doing so may result in legal action.

Currency Exchange: Since not all locations take credit cards, it's a good idea to exchange some money at the border to cover initial costs. Use caution and make sure you get a fair rate while utilizing unreliable money changers. Research the various modes of transit available before crossing borders. Some borders are far away, making it difficult to locate safe transportation. It may be advantageous to hire a local driver or guide.

Security: Research the level of security in the area you intend to visit. Keep aware and use caution as needed because some border regions may be prone to unrest or warfare. Respect regional norms and traditions by acting locally. Smooth border crossings can be greatly facilitated by politeness and friendliness. Keep in mind that every border crossing in West Africa can bring with it specific difficulties and experiences. You can negotiate the complexities of crossing borders in this diverse and exciting region by making plans in advance, keeping yourself informed, and remaining flexible.

Road Trips through West African Landscapes

West Africa's diverse landscapes, cultures, and experiences can be captivatingly explored on a road trip. Here's an illustration of what to expect on this trip: You might begin your tour in Dakar and head east to the vast savannah plains of Senegal. Discover the Fulani herders that wander the area as you pass by the majestic baobab trees in this beautiful setting. The road passes through the endless sand dunes of the Sahara Desert as you enter Mauritania.

While touring the historic city of Chinguetti, set up camp under the starry desert sky. The southern part of Mali, particularly Bamako and Timbuktu, is home to the country's bustling marketplaces. The landscape of the Niger River shifts as you travel from the desert to the lush riverbanks. To get to the intriguing city of Agadez, which is renowned for its mud-brick architecture, continue eastward into Niger's Sahara Desert. The dry splendor of the desert will astound you.

As you move south through Nigeria, you'll come across its stunning rainforests. Visit the country's national parks to observe the wildlife, and explore the energetic cities of Lagos and Abuja. To get to Ivory Coast, which is well-known for its breathtaking beaches, head west along the coast. Experience the vibrant music and dance scene of the country by traveling to Abidjan. Ghanaian

Historical Sites: On a road trip, one can discover Ghana's rich heritage, which includes castles, forts, and the bustling Accra marketplaces. It is worthwhile to explore the slave forts at Cape Coast and Elmina.

Head east into To Visit undiscovered gems such as the Tamberma Valley, which is well-known for its unusual clay-fortified houses. Travelers from further east are drawn to the Abomey royal palaces and Benin's distinctive voodoo culture. Explore the tranquil Lake Nokoué and the stilt settlements.

Go Back to the Coast of Senegal: Return to the coast of Senegal to complete your car trip through West Africa, making stops at Retba Lake and the charming town of Saint-Louis. Remember that a road trip through West Africa is about more than just the landscape; it's also about the locals you meet, the cuisine you sample, and the many cultures that contribute to this region's uniqueness. Read up on travel warnings and prepare for a range of road conditions before embarking on this unusual adventure.

Tales from Travelers on the Trans-West Africa Highway

The Trans-West Africa Highway is a vast network of highways that connects the Sahel to the Atlantic coast and traverses numerous West African nations. People who have traveled this path have related fascinating tales of their experiences, providing a window into the region's rich cultural and geographic diversity.

Saharan Adventures: Passing through Mauritania and Mali on their way north, travelers have awed at the Sahara Desert's size. They share accounts of coming across the nomadic Tuareg tribes, beautiful oases, and never-ending sand dunes. Those who go across this desolate landscape are forever changed by its austere beauty.

Cultural Encounters: The cultural variety of West Africa is well known. Travelers frequently encounter the vivid cultures of numerous ethnic groups along the roadway. These experiences provide a profound understanding for the traditions of the area, from the vibrant festivals of Ghana to the mask dances of Burkina Faso. The vibrant markets of West Africa are a veritable treasure mine of sights, sounds, and tastes. Travelers frequently recount their experiences navigating the maze-like markets, haggling for pricey fabrics in Dakar, Senegal, or trying exotic fruits in Lagos, Nigeria. The route travels through areas rich in history, which is significant historically. Formerly, the great empires of Ghana, Mali, and Songhai were connected through ancient trading routes. The ruins of these civilizations, including the renowned Timbuktu, are explored by tourists who discover the region's significant past.

Road Challenges: Adventure stories wouldn't be complete without descriptions of negotiating difficult driving conditions. Travelers on the roadway must be resourceful and resilient as they navigate everything from potholed roads to river crossings.

Wildlife Wonders: The varied environments of West Africa offer opportunities for wildlife encounters. Travelers frequently recount their experiences seeing elephants in the Pendjari National Park in Burkina Faso or monitoring chimpanzees in the Niokolo-Koba National Park in Senegal. West African food is a culinary joy in and of itself. Travelers delight in the variety of tastes and ingredients particular to each nation, from savory jollof rice to fiery suya skewers.

Warm Hospitality: Many tourists mention how friendly and welcoming the people of West Africa are. The real warmth of the residents makes a lasting impact whether you stay in bustling metropolis or far-flung villages. West Africa has stunning natural scenery, from the dense rainforests of Côte d'Ivoire to the charming coastal beaches of Ghana. Stories of travelers relaxing in these natural havens are common. The Trans-West Africa Highway acts as a bridge between different countries and civilizations.

Many beautiful tales of cross-border friendships and relationships are commonly related by tourists, demonstrating the region's diversity and harmony These accounts from travelers on the Trans-West African Highway not only shed light on West Africa's geography and culture, but they also stoke a desire to travel and an appreciation for the wide range of experiences that this richly varied and dynamic region has to offer.

CHAPTER FIVE

West African Cuisine and Culinary Adventures

Rice, tomatoes, onions, and a variety of spices are combined to make Jollof Rice, a classic West African dish. Each West African country has its unique version of this popular dish.

Suya: A popular street dish, suya consists of grilled and skewered meat, usually beef or chicken, coated with spicy peanut sauce. It's a hot and delicious treat.

Fufu with Egusi Soup: Fufu is a starchy side dish that is commonly served with egusi, a hearty soup made from ground melon seeds. The soup is usually thickened with leafy vegetables and may contain fish or meat.

This Ghanaian dish, known as banku and tilapia, consists of fermented maize and cassava dough (banku) combined with grilled tilapia fish. Hot pepper sauce is often served with it.

Yellow Soup with Achu: Achu is a starchy porridge that is consumed with a vibrant yellow soup that contains spices, groundnuts, and palm fruits. It is a Cameroonian specialty. It's a tasty and unique dish.

Thieboudienne, Senegal's national dish, is made with fish, rice, vegetables, and tomato sauce. It's a flavorful and substantial entrée.

Nigerians love Moin Moin, a steaming bean pudding made with black-eyed peas, onions, peppers, and spices. It's a popular vegetarian option.

Akara: A fried black-eyed pea cake, akaara is a common breakfast or snack in Nigeria. It is soft on the inside and crispy on the outside.

Bissap: A refreshing hibiscus drink that occasionally has pineapple, sugar, or ginger added for taste. In several West African countries, it's a popular beverage.

Plantains: These versatile fruits are often boiled, grilled, or served as a snack or side dish. Try them ripe for sweetness or green for starch.

Remember that every country, and frequently even each region within a country, may have its own unique cuisines and flavors when studying West African cuisine. Be prepared to experience a wide range of sensations, from savory and spicy to sweet and sour, as you embark on your culinary explorations in West Africa.

Exploring Local Markets

In West Africa, local markets are vibrant hubs of the region's cultural and economic life. These markets, which are deeply ingrained in West African traditions, are essential to day-to-day existence. The following is what you should know about them:

Diverse Goods: In West Africa, local markets offer a vast array of goods, including traditional crafts, jewelry, fabrics, clothing, spices, and fresh food. Both locals and tourists can find what they need in these markets. In addition to being places to buy and sell goods, markets in West Africa are important centers of culture. They usually highlight the rich cultural heritage of the region through song, dance, and traditional ceremonies.

Community Gathering: These marketplaces serve as focal points for local get-togethers. People from different towns and villages get together to socialize, trade, and share stories. They are places where neighbors congregate to mingle.

Conventions: Many market operations follow customs and procedures that date back many years. In order to conserve cultural heritage, sellers usually wear traditional clothing and use centuries-old artisan techniques.

Bargaining Culture: Haggling and bargaining are common in West African markets. A fair price is decided through amicable conversations between buyers and sellers. Building relationships is just as important in my practice as doing business.

Local cuisine: West African markets are known for their delicious street food. There are several freshly prepared regional dishes available. You can taste authentic West African flavors with these treats.

These colorful markets are a feast for the senses. The vibrant hues of the crafts and textiles, the sounds of music and conversation, and the aromas of the street food and spices all contribute to a unique and vibrant ambiance. The economies of the West African countries depend heavily on their local markets. At these markets, a large number of people earn a living as food vendors, artisans, and dealers. The informal economy is flourishing in these regions.

Although local markets are rich in customs and culture, they frequently face challenges like inadequate infrastructure, hygienic concerns, and sporadically security threats. To improve the overall market environment, governments and organizations are working to address these issues. Travelers who are keen to experience the local way of life often flock to West African markets. Tourists can enjoy the vibrant environment, purchase unique gifts, and try some of the local cuisine.

Last but not least, West African local markets serve as more than just places to buy and sell goods; they are thriving centers of the arts and economy that provide a glimpse into the customs and culture of the area. The structure of West African societies depends heavily on these markets, which continue to be thriving hubs of activity and commerce.

Bargaining and Shopping Etiquette

Bargaining and shopping etiquette in West Africa, much like in many other parts of the world, involves a set of cultural norms and practices that are important to understand when visiting the region. Here are some key points to keep in mind:

Politeness and Respect: Politeness is highly valued in West African cultures. When bargaining, always approach vendors with respect and a friendly demeanor. Greet them warmly and ask about their day or family before discussing prices.

Haggling is Expected: Bargaining is a common practice in West African markets. Vendors often set their initial prices higher than what they expect to receive, so negotiation is expected. Be prepared to haggle, but do so in a friendly and respectful manner.

Start with a Smile: Begin the bargaining process with a smile and a compliment about the product. This helps build rapport and can lead to a more favorable price.

Know the Market Value: Before you start bargaining, it's important to have a rough idea of the market value of the item you're interested in. This will help you determine a fair price and avoid overpaying.

Be Patient: Bargaining can be a lengthy process. Don't rush it. Take your time, have some patience, and enjoy the interaction with the vendor.

Walk Away if Necessary: If you're unable to reach a price that you find reasonable, it's okay to walk away. Often, this can lead to the vendor offering a better deal to keep your business.

Respect Local Customs: Be mindful of local customs and traditions. Some items may have cultural or spiritual significance, so be respectful when bargaining for them.

Handle Bargaining with Tact: Avoid being overly aggressive or confrontational during bargaining. It's important to maintain a friendly and cooperative attitude throughout the process.

Inspect Goods Carefully: Before finalizing a purchase, inspect the item closely to ensure it meets your expectations in terms of quality and condition. If there are any issues, negotiate accordingly.

Payment Methods: Cash is often the preferred method of payment in many West African markets. Make sure you have small denominations of local currency, as change may be limited.

Be Mindful of Personal Space: In crowded markets, personal space can be limited. Be respectful of the personal space of others and be cautious with your belongings to prevent theft.

Enjoy the Experience: Shopping in West Africa is not just about acquiring goods; it's also about the experience. Engage with the local vendors, learn about their crafts, and immerse yourself in the culture.

Dress Appropriately: When visiting markets and local shops, it's a good idea to dress modestly and respectfully, especially if you're in a more conservative region. This shows respect for local customs and can help you blend in more easily.

Learn Basic Local Phrases: While English or French may be spoken in many West African countries, learning a few basic local phrases in the native language can go a long way in building rapport with vendors. Simple greetings and polite phrases can be very appreciated.

Support Local Artisans: West Africa is known for its rich tradition of craftsmanship. When shopping for souvenirs or handmade goods, prioritize purchasing from local artisans and craftspeople. This supports the local economy and helps preserve traditional skills.

Ask for Permission to Take Photos: If you want to take photos of vendors or their products, it's polite to ask for their permission first. Some vendors may not want their products or themselves photographed.

Be Mindful of Bargaining in Tourist Areas: In touristy regions, prices may be inflated. It's even more important to negotiate in such areas, but remember to be fair and respectful in your haggling.

Try Local Foods: Don't forget to explore the local food markets and street vendors. Trying local dishes is an integral part of the cultural experience. Ask locals for recommendations on where to find the best local cuisine.

Be Aware of Local Holidays: Markets and shops may have different hours or be closed during local holidays and festivals. Check ahead of time to avoid disappointment.

Leave No Trace: If you visit remote or natural areas to shop for unique items, be environmentally conscious.

Don't leave trash behind, and respect the environment and local wildlife.

Negotiate for Services: Bargaining isn't limited to just physical goods. You can also negotiate prices for services like transportation, guided tours, or even accommodations in some cases.

Don't Feel Obligated: While it's nice to support local businesses, don't feel obligated to make a purchase if you're not genuinely interested in the product. Polite refusal is acceptable.

Ask for Directions: If you're unfamiliar with the area, don't hesitate to ask locals for directions or recommendations. They can often provide valuable insights on where to find the best deals or hidden gems. Remember that shopping and bargaining in West Africa is not just about transactions; it's an opportunity to connect with local culture, build relationships, and gain a deeper understanding of the region. Approach it with an open mind and a spirit of adventure.

Cultural Significance of Meals

In West Africa, meals play a significant cultural role that reflects the region's rich heritage, diversity of ethnic groups, and traditions. The cultural significance of meals in West Africa can be summed up in the following ways: Sharing meals is a crucial aspect of West African culture, which emphasizes hospitality and community. Guests are frequently treated with the highest consideration and generosity, and shared meals strengthen ties between relatives and friends.

Traditional Food: The variety of flavors and ingredients in West African food is well-known. Commonly utilized staples include rice, yams, cassava, and plantains. The meals are given depth by the use of herbs, spices, and chili peppers, making for a distinctive dining experience.

Symbolism: Many dishes from West Africa have symbolic ingredients. For instance, during rituals or gatherings, the Kola nut is sometimes offered as a symbol of welcome and solidarity. In different cultural situations, some dishes also have particular connotations. West Africans celebrate significant life events with special meals as part of rituals and ceremonies. Traditional foods cooked with care are frequently served at births, weddings, and funerals. These dinners foster generational interaction and cultural legacy preservation.

Elders and Family: In West African culture, the family is of utmost importance. Family members gather around the table for meals to tell tales, pass on customs, and generally spend time together. Traditionally, elders are served first to show respect for their experience and knowledge.

Festivals & Religious Observances: Many religious ceremonies and festivals in West Africa involve eating and the cooking of certain foods. These celebrations bring people together to honor their common cultural and religious practices.

Meals are frequently accompanied by music and dance. To create a festive ambiance, traditional instruments like drums and xylophones are used, enhancing the dining experience's cultural diversity.

Gender Roles: There are certain gender roles linked with food preparation in several West African communities. Although women frequently rule the kitchen, men may play a part in the preparation of food or in activities like hunting and gathering.

Soul Food: The culinary traditions of the African diaspora, notably in the Americas, have been influenced by West African cuisine. Foods like fried plantains, gumbo, and jollof rice are popular worldwide and help individuals connect to their West African heritage. Traditional foods are still important, but West African cuisine has evolved to reflect contemporary preferences and lifestyles. Fusion and West African-inspired fast food restaurants are growing in popularity.

In conclusion, meals in West Africa are more than just fuel for the body; they are a representation of social ties, history, and cultural values. They foster community, honor heritage, and add to the lively cultural identity of the area.

CHAPTER SIX

Vibrant Urban Marvels Cities and Accommodation

Lagos, Nigeria and Accommodation

Lagos, the largest city in Nigeria, is also one of the cities with the greatest population growth. It is a dynamic metropolis renowned for its vibrant street life, music culture, and thriving Nollywood film industry. The city is a center for commerce, innovation, and technology.

Accommodation

Eko Hotel & Suites

The secret to Eko Hotels & Suites' success in West Africa is the proper combination. With dining and recreational options subtly incorporated into one stunning location, its clients enjoy the ideal combination of business and leisure services right in the center of Victoria Island. This provides services that are up to the highest international standards to top all of these.

An 8-minute walk from Kuramo Beach on the Gulf of Guinea, this relaxed hotel is 6 km from the Nigerian National Museum and 31 km from Murtala Muhammed International Airport. Airy rooms with balconies and wood floors offer free Wi-Fi, flat-screen TVs and safes. Upgraded rooms add minifridges, and tea and coffee making equipment; some have garden views. Suites feature separate living areas. Upgraded suites provide Nespresso machines and panoramic views. Amenities include 5 restaurants, a cafe and 2 bars, as well as an outdoor pool, a gym, a tennis court and a spa. Meeting and event space is also available.

Address: 1415 Adetokunbo Ademola Street, Victoria Island, Lagos 106104, Lagos
Phone: 0708 070 0545
Check-in time: 14:00
Check-out time: 12:00

Phone / Fax
- **International Calls:** +234 201 2772700
- **National Calls**: 0201 2772700

- **E-mail:** sales@ekohotels.com, reservation@ekohotels.com, banquet@ekohotels.com

Wheatbaker Hotel

The Wheatbaker Hotel The Wheatbaker, a spa and health center in Lagos, has an outdoor pool with sun loungers. There is free Wi-Fi available everywhere. Every air-conditioned room has a safety deposit box and a coffee maker. Private bathrooms come equipped with a shower or bathtub and a hair dryer. The on-site restaurant serves both local and international food. The bar serves a variety of drinks.

The Wheatbaker is 30 kilometers away from Murtala Muhammed International Airport.

Address: 4 Lawrence Rd, Ikoyi, Lagos 101233, Lagos
Phone: 0809 522 4444

Most Popular Facilities
- Indoor swimming pool

- Free WiFi
- Airport Shuttle
- Fitness Centre
- Free Parking
- Family Rooms
- Spa and Wellness Centre
- Non-smoking Rooms
- Bar
- Exceptional Breakfast
- Property Highlights

Check-in: From 14:00

Check-out: From 02:00 to 11:00

Age restriction: The minimum age for check-in is **18**

Pets: Pets are not allowed.

Top attractions
- Freedom Park Lagos - 6 km
- Iga Idungaran-OBA Of Lagos Palace - 8 km
- Lekki Conservation Centre

Radisson Blu Anchorage Hotel

Welcome to the luxurious and comfortable Radisson Blu Anchorage Hotel in Lagos, V.I. From here, visitors take in picturesque views of the developing city. A variety of remarkable services are available at this hotel to ensure that your stay is one to remember. Savor the luxuriously furnished suites, top-notch dining options, cutting-edge exercise facility, and tranquil spa.

The devoted staff is committed to provide individualized service to satisfy all of your needs, whether you are here on business or for pleasure. Make your reservation now to enjoy unmatched hospitality.

Address: 1a Ozumba Mbadiwe Ave, Victoria Island, Lagos 101241, Lagos
Check-in: 2:00pm
Check-out: 12:00pm

Contact
- +234708 061 0000
- +234 8 139 850 600

- +2348 139 850 600
- info.lagos@radissonblu.com
- +234 (0)14 610 126

Nearby Attractions

- **Kalakuta Republic Museum:** 12.39 mi / 19.93 km from the hotel
- **Nike Centre for Art and Culture:** 4.46 mi / 7.18 km from the hotel
- **The Cathedral Church of Christ:** 2.09 mi / 3.36 km from the hotel
- **Hans & Rene Ice Cream Shop:** 2.65 mi / 4.27 km from the hotel
- **Tafawa Balewa Square:** 1.22 mi / 1.96 km from the hotel
- **Victoria Island**: 0.69 mi / 1.11 km from the hotel

Accessibility

- Concierge service
- Executive business lounge
- Fitness center
- Spa

- Airport shuttle
- Bar
- Breakfast buffet
- Express check-out
- Free Wi-Fi
- Grab & Go Breakfast
- Hair salon
- Hybrid Meeting
- Safety deposit box
- Laundry service
- Luggage storage
- Meeting facilities
- Minibar or fridge
- On-site dining
- On-site restaurant(s)
- Outdoor pool
- Parking
- Room service

Federal Palace Hotel & Casino

Overlooking Lagos Lagoon, this high-end hotel is 2 km from the Nigerian National Museum and 3 km from Freedom Park. Featuring plush furnishings, the polished, modern rooms offer free Wi-Fi, flat-screen TVs, minibars, desks, and tea and coffee making facilities. Upgraded rooms add lagoon views. Refined 1- and 2-bedroom suites add living/dining areas. Room service is available. With an award-winning venue, the Federal Palace Hotel and Casino has won the Lagos State Lotteries Board Outstanding Contribution Award in the casino category, demonstrating its enormous impact on the city's gaming sector.

With a choice of eleven conference and meeting rooms, the Federal Palace is among the top conference locations in Lagos, adding a sophisticated, businesslike touch to any event. The Federal Palace is equipped to accommodate a variety of events, from intimate gatherings to major conferences, and guarantees that your event will go smoothly.

Address: 6-8 Ahmadu Bello Way, Victoria Island, Lagos 101241, Lagos

Phone: 0201 277 9000

Website: reservations@federalpalace.com

Check-in time: 14:00

Check-out time: 11:00

Amenities

- Free Wi-Fi
- Free breakfast
- Free parking
- Air-conditioned
- Outdoor Pool
- Restaurant
- Gym
- Internet in room
- Seaside

Lagos Oriental Hotel

Situated on the banks of Five Cowries Creek with a view of Lagos Island, this upscale hotel is 5 km from the Nigerian National Museum and 2 km from Bar Beach's white sands. The sleek, well-appointed rooms offer flat-screen TVs, Wi-Fi, minifridges, and tea and coffee makers; some have views of the water. Some upgraded rooms have separate living rooms and minibars, while others have safes and sitting places. Room service is available all day and all night. There is a coffee shop, a bar/lounge, and a classy Asian restaurant. A business center, a gym, and an outdoor pool with a view of the creek are among the other facilities.

Address: 3 Lekki Epe Expy Road, Victoria Island, Lagos, 106104, Nigeria.

Contact Information
12806600
+234 702 696 00 65

Info: fo@lagosoriental.com
Website: www.lagosoriental.com
Check-in time: 15:00
Check-out time: 00:00

Popular Amenities

- Pool
- Spa
- Breakfast
- free
- Wi-Fi
- free

Four Points by Sheraton

This elegant hotel is located 6 kilometers from the Nigerian National Museum, 4 km from the upscale Ikoyi neighborhood, and 2 km from the Gulf of Guinea. Contemporary tiled rooms come equipped with minifridges, flat-screen TVs, tea and coffee makers, safes, and Wi-Fi (charge); some even have iPod docks. Suites have balconies, while executive rooms have views of the top level. Room service is offered all day and all night.

There is a sophisticated Asian restaurant, a sports bar, an outdoor lounge, a lobby cafe, and a French brasserie with checkered floors that serves buffet-style meals. In addition, there are eight meeting rooms, an indoor pool, a spa, and a gym.

Address: Plot 9/10 Block 2 Oniru Chieftaincy Estate, Victoria Island, Lagos 021189, Lagos

Phone: 0905 382 2225

Check-in: 3:00 pm

Check-out: 12:00 pm

See Accessibility Features

Pet Policy

Pets Not Allowed

Featured Amenities On -site
- Free Wifi
- Restaurant
- Bar
- Indoor Pool
- Fitness Center
- Meeting Space
- Convenience Store
- Dry Cleaning Service

- Laundry
- Hair salon
- Room Service
- Wake up Calls
- 24 Hour Room Service
- Daily Housekeeping
- Mobile Key
- Digital Check In

The landmark Victoria Island hotel

This laid-back hotel is located across the Atlantic Ocean from Landmark Beach, 5 km from the Nike Art Gallery, and 29 km from Murtala Muhammed International Airport. The cozy accommodations have minifridges, Wi-Fi, and smart TVs. Room upgrades include balconies, sitting places, and/or views of the ocean. There are dining rooms and kitchens in the flats.

Address: 5b Water Corporation Road Oniru Estate, Lagos 106104, Nigeria.
Phone: 0903 949 2427

Email:

hotels@landmarkafrica.com

contactus@landmarkafrica.comAmenities

Check-in: from 14:00 until 21:00

Check-out: from 06:00 until 12:00

Amenities

- An outdoor pool,
- A gym
- A spa
- A beachfront restaurant
- Parking is available.

Lagos Continental Hotel

This luxurious, high-rise hotel is located in the Victoria Island district, 10 kilometers from the National Arts Theatre and 4 km from Ikoyi neighborhood shops. Free Wi-Fi, flat-screen TVs, iPod docks, and sofas are all features of the modern, stylish rooms with floor-to-ceiling windows and city views. Whirlpool baths are available in certain rooms, and suites offer more living space. A spa and a rooftop pool are among the facilities. There are other modern dining options as well.

Address: 52a Kofo Abayomi St, Victoria Island, Lagos 101241, Lagos, Nigeria.
Phone: +234 (0) 2012366666
Email: info@thelagoscontinental.com

Ghana's Capital, Accra, and Accommodation

Ghana's capital, Accra, is located on West Africa's Atlantic coast. Ghana's first president, who played a key role in guiding the nation toward independence, is honored at Kwame Nkrumah Memorial Park. Nkrumah's mausoleum and a museum detailing his life are located in the park. The city's expansive, vibrant market is called Makola Market. Well-known beaches with golden sand and a vibrant nightlife are Labadi Beach and Kokrobite Beach.

Population: 284,124
Area: 225.7 km^2

Area code: 030

Demonym: Accran

Elevation: 61 m (200 ft)

Postcode Districts: GA, GL, GZ

Region: Greater Accra Region

Best Hotels in Ghana

The 5-star Mövenpick Ambassador Hotel

The Movenpick Ambassador Hotel Accra is located in the business district/city center, in an urban paradise. Located just 7km from the airport, this modern 5-star hotel offers free WiFi and a free airport shuttle, making it your home away from home while visiting Accra. With free coffee and tea, 46-inch TVs, laptop-sized safes, and in-room ironing facilities, the contemporary rooms and suites provide breathtaking views of the garden or the city. The African art collection, which features more than 2500 original works of art, is available to guests throughout the hotel. For a little more, visitors can opt for the Executive Club Floor, which features a boardroom, a private lounge with a balcony, and private check-in and check-out.

114

In an intimate "home away from home" setting, savor complimentary evening canapes with a selection of wines and champagne while admiring the opulent grounds. A la Carte, international buffets, and light snacks are among the many eating options offered. The ground floor conference facilities, which include a 736 square meter ballroom with five adjoining meeting rooms, a business center, and a sizable pre-function area, are perfect for planning social or professional gatherings. You can brace yourself in Accra's largest outdoor swimming pool or work out at the state-of-the-art gymnasium. The hotel's Emporium features a number of stores and establishments, such as a bank and ATM, a pharmacy, a computer and cell phone store, and a hair and beauty parlor.

Address: Ridge, Pmb Ct 343, Independence Ave, Accra, Ghana
Phone: +233 30 261 1000
Email: hotel.accra.reservations@movenpick.com

Kempinski Hotel Gold Coast City Accra

This luxurious hotel, housed in a modern glass and concrete structure, is 2 km from the eateries and bars of bustling Oxford Street and 11 minutes' walk from the Accra International Conference Centre. The well-kept rooms have Ghanaian artwork, wooden flooring, and windows that reach the ceiling. They have flat-screen TVs, minibars, free Wi-Fi, workstations, safes, and sitting places. Nespresso machines and separate sitting areas are features of suites. 24/7 room service is available.

Breakfast is complimentary. There are three stylish bars and a contemporary Mediterranean restaurant with an open kitchen for dining and drinking. In addition, there is a gym, a spa, and an outdoor pool. Located in Accra's Galleria

Address: Ministries PMB, 66 Gamel Abdul Nasser Ave, Accra, Ghana

Phone: +233 24 243 6000

Email: reservations.accra@kempinski.com

Check-in time: 15:00

Check-out time: 12:00

The Labadi Beach Hotel

This luxurious hotel on Labadi Beach, surrounded by tropical gardens, is 7 kilometers from the vibrant Accra city center and 8 km from Kwame Nkrumah Memorial Park's tomb and museum. The stylish, modern rooms have minibars, tea and coffee makers, free Wi-Fi, and flat-screen TVs. Upgrades include Nespresso machines, and all have balconies. Upgrades include kitchenettes; posh suites contain living and dining spaces. Room service is offered all day and all night.

Parking is free, and breakfast is provided in a classy restaurant. Additionally, there is a cocktail lounge, a piano bar, and a balcony with a view of an outdoor pool. A sauna and a meeting room are among the facilities.

Address: Number one, La Rd, Accra, Ghana

Phone: +233 30 274 2060

Check-in time: 14:00

Check-out time: 12:0

Price: $292.31

Website: https://labadibeachhotelgh.com/

Accra Marriott Hotel

This classy hotel is located 8km from Labadi Beach and 9km from the Achimota Forest, and it's a 14-minute walk from Kotoka International Airport. Streamlined rooms come equipped with minibars, safes, private bathrooms, tea and coffee makers, flat-screen TVs, and complimentary Wi-Fi. Access to the executive lounge and patio is available in certain upgraded rooms. There is room service available. Breakfast, parking, and airport transfers are all free extras. Two elegant restaurants, one with poolside seating, a bar, and an outdoor pool are also available. A fitness center, barbecues, and an executive lounge with a patio are additional features. There is space for an event.

Address: Liberation Road Airport City, Accra, Ghana
Phone: +233 30 273 8000
Check-in time: 15:00
Check-out time: 12:00
Instagram: marriottbonvoy

Dakar, Senegal and Accommodation

Senegal's capital, Dakar, is located in West Africa. Situated on the Cap-Vert peninsula, it is an Atlantic port. The Grande Mosquée, distinguished by a tall minaret, is located in the city's ancient Médina neighborhood. Clothes, drums, carvings, and tools are among the cultural objects on display at the Musée Théodore Monod. The native mbalax music serves as an inspiration for the city's thriving nightlife.

Population: 3,540,000

Area: 83 km²

Elevation: 22 m (72 ft)

Settled: 15th century

Best Hotels in Dakar,

Radisson Blu Hotel, Dakar Sea Plaza

This contemporary beachside hotel is 3 km from Îles des Madeleines national park and 12 km from Léopold Sédar Senghor International Airport. Polished rooms feature complimentary Wi-Fi, as well as flat-screen TVs, minibars and coffeemakers; some provide sea views. Upgraded rooms offer Nespresso machines and breakfast. Suites add living areas, while enhanced suites feature kitchens, terraces and whirlpool spas.

Parking is complimentary. There's a fine Mediterranean bistro, an Asian restaurant, and a poolside cocktail bar serving nibbles. Other amenities include a fitness center, a spa and an infinity pool overlooking the ocean.

Address: Rte de la Corniche O, Dakar 16868, Senegal
+221 33 869 33 33
Price: $262.59
Website: www.radissonhotels.com
Check-in time: 14:00
Check-out time: 12:00
Pullman Dakar Teranga
Across the road from the Atlantic Ocean, this premium hotel is a 13-minute walk from the IFAN Museum of African Arts and 2 miles from the Grand Mosque of Dakar. Modern rooms provide free Wi-Fi, flat-screen TVs, minibars, and city or ocean views, as well as tea

and coffee making facilities. Upgraded rooms offer balconies. Dining options include a patio brasserie close to an outdoor pool, as well as an upscale French restaurant/bar. There's also a private beach, a hammam and a gym. Parking is available.

Price: $252.93

Address: Place de l'Independance, 10 Rue PL 29, Dakar 10200, Senegal

Contact: +221 33 889 22 00

Check-in time: 14:00

Check-out time: 12:00

GPS:14.667778, -17.431611

Email:dakar.reservation@accor.com

Novotel Dakar

This hotel is Opposite a strip of sandy beach along the Atlantic Ocean, this casual hotel is a 13-minute walk from the Place de l'Independance and 1 km from the Musée Théodore Monod's African art shows. Simple rooms offer flat-screen TVs and safes, as well as tea and coffee making facilities, and complimentary Wi-Fi.

Upgraded accommodations add sitting spaces and/or ocean views. Parking is complimentary. Breakfast (fee) is offered at an unfussy restaurant. There are also 2 stylish bars providing snacks, and an outdoor pool.

Address: Avenue Abdoulaye Fadiga, BP 2073
18524 DAKAR, Senegal
GPS:14.668828, -17.426773Check-in time: 12:00
Check-out time: 12:00
Contact: +221 33 849 49 94
Email: dakar.reservation@accor.com
Price: $165.62

Freetown, Sierra Leone and Accommodation

Freetown, the capital of Sierra Leone, is a port city located in West Africa. It is well-known for its beaches and its part in the slave traffic across the Atlantic. A symbol of emancipation is the centuries-old Cotton Tree in the old town. Previously enslaved people walked to freedom through the King's Yard Gate on the waterfront.

The 19th-century military leader Bai Bureh is the subject of exhibitions at the Sierra Leone National Museum.

District: Western Area Urban District

Elevation: 26 m (85 ft)

Founded: March 11, 1792

The Lead Hotel

On a white sand beach, next to Sierra Leone's historic landmark, the "Man of War Bay," is where you'll find the Lead Hotel. The Lead Hotel, located in the middle of Aberdeen, Freetown's commercial and tourist hub, is the only apartment hotel in Freetown, Sierra Leone, with a private beach. Situated in the center of a peaceful private harbor with a view of the Atlantic Ocean, The Lead Hotel is impromptu near the center of everything. Surrounded by all those famous eateries, it is a ten-minute walk to the golf club and a one-minute stroll to the well-known Lumley Beach. Tuk-tuks, taxis, and shuttle buses are constantly available for a short ride (no more than 20 minutes) to the city center. River Number Two Beach, the National Museum, and Tacugama are all within a half-hour's drive. In addition to being easy to get there, the Lead Hotel is also easily accessible. Once you arrive at Freetown Lungi International Airport, you can be dropped off at the pier on the hotel grounds by private boat. Alternatively, you can use a shuttle bus or a water taxi to get to the hotel in about 30 minutes.

Address : 72a Cape Rd, Freetown, Sierra Leone

Phone: +232 33 933333

E-mail: info@livingthelead.com

Price: $267.52

Check-in time: 14:00

Check-out time: 12:00

Hotel Barmoi - Best Hotel at Freetown in Sierra Leone

This little hotel is located 650m from Lumley Beach road on a peninsula with a view of the Atlantic Ocean. It is 3km from Lumley Beach and 8km from the iconic Cotton Tree in Freetown. Elegant rooms with air conditioning, TVs, minifridges, and free Wi-Fi are available, some with lounge areas. There are several with private balconies overlooking the ocean. All have private bathrooms.

There's a laid-back eatery/bar with brunch. Additionally, there is a patio overlooking the ocean and an outdoor pool. Space is available for an event.

Address : 75C Cape Road, Freetown, Sierra Leone
Phone: +232 30 960016
Email:enquiries@hotelbarmoi.com
Price: $118.08
Check-in time: 15:00
Check-out time: 12:00

Sierra Palms Resort
The Sierra Palms Resort is located 8.3 km from the Sierra Leone National Museum and 29 km from the Western Area Forest Reserve. Lungi International Airport, which is 35 kilometers from the hotel, is the closest airport. It provides lodging with a garden, a shared lounge, free private parking, and an outdoor pool. In addition to having access to a balcony and a private

beach area, each room at the four-star hotel offers views of the city. The lodging offers free WiFi all across the property, room service, airport shuttles, and a front desk staffed around-the-clock. Air-conditioned rooms with a desk, kettle, refrigerator, minibar, safety deposit box, flat-screen TV, patio, and private bathroom with bidet will be available to visitors at the hotel. The rooms at Sierra Palms Resort come with towels and bed linens.

There are continental, Italian, and American breakfast options offered every morning. There is a restaurant in the lodging that serves Chinese, American, and African food. Vegan, halal, and vegetarian choices are also available upon request. The business center offers an ATM, a fax machine, a photocopy, and a tour desk. Car rentals are also offered.

Address : 75 Lumley Beach Rd, Freetown, Sierra Leone
Phone: +232 80 222222
Price: $147.06
Check-in time: 12:00
Check-out time: 11:00

Pearl Hotel

The Pearl Hotel & Residence is a calm haven where you may relax by the pool or in the garden. Convenient and comfortable, this sanctuary has a coffee shop, free English breakfast, and laundry facilities nearby.

Address: FPC9+78C, Freetown, Sierra Leone

Phone: +232 77 200202

Check-out time: 11:00

Price: $255.70

Amenities

- Bar
- Airport transfer
- Lounge area
- Pool
- Gym
- Free breakfast

What's nearby

- Lumley Beach - 9 min walk
- National Stadium - 9 min drive
- Cotton Tree - 9 min drive

- Sierra Leone National Museum - 9 min drive
- State House - 9 min drive

Banjul, The Gambia: and Accommodation

The capital of the Gambia, a small West African nation bounded by Senegal, is Banjul. At the meeting point of the Atlantic Ocean and the Gambia River, the city is situated on an island. The Gambia differs from many other places in certain ways. Major European locations are only six hours away, there is no jet lag, and it is a well-liked and reasonably priced winter vacation spot that draws travelers seeking sun, sea, sand, and cultural experiences all of which this unusual nation has in abundance. Among its colonial structures is the National Museum, which honors Gambian history and culture. Colorful fabrics and regional produce are sold by vendors in the bustling Albert Market. The massive Arch 22 doorway, with its many columns, marks the city's primary entrance.

Division: Banjul

Elevation: 0 m (0 ft)

Founded: 23 April 1816 as Bathurst

Accommodation

Bojang River Lodge

Bakau, The Gambia's Cape Point beach is home to the quaint Bojang River Lodge. Three superior rooms, two one-bedroom suites, two two-bedroom flats, and six ordinary rooms are among the many lodging choices it provides. The hotel also features a pool bar, restaurant, and swimming pool.

For a quick vacation or a romantic retreat, Bojang River Lodge is ideal. For weddings, family gatherings, or long Gambia holidays, it's also a fantastic option.

In addition to the hotel's lovely location and breathtaking sea views, the staff is warm and inviting.

Check-out time: 11:00

Address: F8JP+R45, off Kofi Annan Street, Bakau, Gambia

Phone: +220 202 2988

Price: $44.43

Services & Amenities

- Linen & Towels Changed
- Cleaning Service
- WiFi
- Beauty Treatments (appt only)
- Private Events
- Pool Table
- Swimming Pool
- Airport Pick Up

Majula Boutique Hotel

In the center of Fajara, directly on the beach, is a brand-new boutique hotel in a genuinely iconic setting. The Majula provides a very remarkable experience. With a huge pool, great food and drink, a sky spa, incredibly attentive staff, and much more.

Address: 62 Atlantic Blvd, Serrekunda, Gambia

Phone: +220 224 4400

Price: $188.74

Check-in time: 14:00

Check-out time: 12:00

Amenities

- Pool
- Parking
- Wi-Fi
- Air conditioning
- Internet
- Wellness
- Restaurant
- Parking & transport

Tamala Beach Resort

This chic hotel is located 19 km from Banjul International Airport on a beautiful Atlantic Ocean beach in a tourist-heavy neighborhood. The cozy rooms have flat-screen TVs, sitting spaces, furnished patios, Wi-Fi, and four-poster mattresses with mosquito nets. They also have tea and coffee makers and minifridges. Upgraded accommodations have terraces with direct access to a common pool and/or views of the ocean.

Address: Serrekunda, Gambia

Phone: +220 732 7777

WhatsApp Number: +220 7327777

Email: info@tamalaresort.com

Check-in time: 14:00

Check-out time: 12:00

Popular amenities

- Spa
- Parking
- Breakfast
- Internet
- Wi-Fi
- Front desk
- 24-hour
- Full-service laundry
- Parking & transport
- Airport shuttle

- Restaurant
- Bar
- Room service

Closed Attraction
- Kotu Beach
- Banjul International Airport
- Kotu Area
- Residential Area
- Market Places
- Tanji Bird Reserve

Cotonou, Benin and Accommodation

Benin's south coast is home to the sizable port city of Cotonou in West Africa. The massive Dantokpa Market, which is located at the eastern end of central Boulevard St. Michel, sells both commonplace products and holy articles and spices. A remarkable red-and-white striped facade may be seen on the southwest side of the 19th-century Cotonou Cathedral. Modern African art can be seen nearby at the Fondation Zinsou museum in the Haie Vive neighborhood.

Area: 79 km²

Elevation: 51 m

Neighborhoods: Fidjrossè, Agla, Menontin, Vedoko, Zogbo

Best Hotel Cotonou, Benin,

Sofitel Cotonou Marina Hotel & Spa

The Sofitel Cotonou Marina Hotel & Spa is a distinctive luxury treasure located in the center of Benin, just a short distance from the beach. With well-appointed rooms and suites, flexible meeting spaces, and the city's largest hotel convention center, this recently opened five-star hotel embraces modernity. The villa has two swimming pools, three concept restaurants, two tennis courts, and a 1000-square-meter spa. Guests can also opt for a private pool villa for a more tranquil getaway.

The Sofitel Cotonou Marina Hotel & Spa is well situated to host meetings and explore Benin, just five minutes from the Cotonou International Airport. The hotel is conveniently located within 15 minutes of Cotonou's main attractions, such as the Danktopa Market, Fidjrossè, and the Institut Français du Bénin, and is easily accessible by automobile.

Address: 1820 Boulevard de la Marina, 081 BP 7300 Cotonou Aeroport
Phone: +229 21 36 60 00
GPS:6.351063, 2.3934
Price: 482896
Email: HB845@sofitel.com
Check-in time: 14:00
Check-out time: 12:00

Popular Amenities
- Air Conditioning
- Coffeemaker
- Mini-Bar
- Rooms for Non-smokers

- Telephone
- Safe (In Room)
- Cable/Satellite Television
- Television
- Internet Access (Wireless)

Golden Tulip Diplomate Cotonou

Situated next to government offices, this elegant hotel is 5 km from Cotonou International Airport and a 5-minute walk from Erevan Beach on the Atlantic Ocean. The well-lit, well-appointed rooms come equipped with minifridges, flat-screen TVs, safes, tea & coffee makers, and complimentary Wi-Fi. Espresso machines are included in the upgraded rooms. Suites have private living spaces, views of the ocean, and some even have whirlpool spas.

Breakfast and parking are free. There are also three bars, a casino, and a formal restaurant with floor-to-ceiling windows. A fitness center, a hot tub, and an outdoor pool are also available.

Address: N° 90 rue 12.017 - Boulevard de la Marina, 01 Bp 8379 Cotonou, Benin

Phone: +229 21 30 02 00

Booking contact: (+33) 1 70 98 61 18

Price: 215740

E-mail : info@goldentuplediplomatecotonou.com

Check-in time: 14:00

Check-out time: 12:00

Types of cooking

- ★ International
- ★ Full American Buffet Breakfast
- ★ Children's menu
- ★ Special Allergy Menu
- ★ Specific Hallah menu
- ★ Special Vegetarian Menu

Beach Sand Hotel & Resort

The Standard Rooms, Superior Suite, Prestige Suite, Executive Suite, and Royal Suite are among the well-kept and opulently decorated rooms and suites of this lovely hotel in Cotonou, all of which are furnished with the newest conveniences. You will sense the hotel's unique, cozy environment as soon as you walk in, which will make you feel at home. You will feel relaxed and at ease at the Beach Sand Hotel because of its unique charm and cozy atmosphere. In addition to being only 150 meters from the beach, it offers convenient access to shops, entertainment, and companies.

Address: Carré 93 Finangnon, Zone des Ambassades Akpakpa, Cotonou, Republic of Bénin.
Price: 115069
Check-in time: 08:00
Check-out time: 00:00
Phone: +229 53 64 91 65
Contact Info: reserve@beachsandhotel.com
http://www.beachsandhotel.com/

Ouagadougou, Burkina Faso and Accommodation

As early as 1050 CE, the Soninke Wangara diaspora from the Ghana Empire established the city. The name Wagadugu, which translates to "home of the Wagu," was renamed Ouagadougou in French.

The capital of Burkina Faso, Ouagadougou, also known as Wagadugu, serves as the country's administrative, communications, cultural, and economic hub. Its Population is **3,359,000.** It is also the biggest city in the nation. They are known as Ouagalais and the area is 219.3 km².

Best Hotels in Ouagadougou, Burkina
Bravia Hotel Ouagadougou

The hotel offers a pick-up and drop-off service at the airport and is conveniently located near it. It is secure and near Ouagadougou's equivalent of a high street. The restaurant, the reception, and the guest relations manager are all quite welcoming. The rooms are nicely furnished with fine furnishings, toiletries, and other amenities. Additionally, there are two ATMs outside the hotel and one inside, making the stay safer and more pleasant.

Address: 9F6M+5JG, Sector 4, District ZACA, Koulouba, Ouagadougou, Burkina Faso
Phone : +226 25 32 97 97
Email.com: braviahotel@gmail.com
Price: 327987

Pros

- ❖ Just besides the airport
- ❖ Free shuttle service
- ❖ Plenty of vegetarian options to eat
- ❖ Good security
- ❖ Jet spray in washroom
- ❖ Proper plugs

Cons

- Mosquitoes in the restaurant
- Dim lighting in restaurant

Property Amenities

→ Free parking

→ Free High Speed Internet (WiFi)

→ Fitness Center with Gym / Workout Room

→ Pool

→ Free breakfast

→ Aerobics

→ Tennis court offsite

→ Kids stay freeLancaster Ouaga 2000

Room features

- Blackout curtains

- Bathrobes

- Air conditioning

- Housekeeping

- Room service

- Coffee / tea maker

- Cable / satellite TV

- Bath / showerSonia Hotels Ouagadougou

Sopatel Silmande Hôtel

The hotel has a fantastic view of the park and lake from its sides and is situated in a calm and peaceful area. Airport transportation is provided by the hotel. The hotel's soft landscape and swimming pool, which is undergoing repair, are well-managed to create the full resort experience.

Address: 9FRX+P43, N3, Ouagadougou, Burkina Faso
Phone: +226 25 35 62 62
Check-in time: 12:00
Check-out time: 12:00

What's nearby

- Faso Parc: 900 m
- Parc Bangr Weogo: 1.6 km
- National Museum of Music: 3.1 km
- Espace or: 3 km
- Jardin lAmitié Ouaga: 3.4 km
- Faso Loisirs 4.4km

Ramada Pearl Hotel

The Ramada Pearl Hotel Guangzhou by Wyndham brand is situated next to the serene Pearl River, close to Guangzhou's Consulate Area and Central Business District. Guangzhou-Kowloon Express Railway Station is 5 km away, Canton Tower and Haixinsha Asian Games Park are 1 kilometer away, the US Consulate is 1.3 km away, Baiyun International Airport is 35 km away, and the Guangzhou International Convention Exhibition Center is 8 km away. There are many different dining options available to guests, including Western buffets and fixed meals as well as regional Chinese cuisine.

Phone: (+226) 25650301/78839283
(+226) 25650300/74942072
Address: 9F7M+M56, Koulouba, Ouagadougou, Burkina Faso
Contact Info: reservation@ramadapearl-hotel.com

Royal Beach Hotel Ouagadougou

The hotel is security conscious, the staff handles this with a smile and without aggression. The closest beach is fifteen hours' driving from the Royal Beach Hotel. You feel secure inside the hotel, which is encircled by walls and fencing. From the comfort of your accommodation, you will observe the daily activities of the Ouaga people, making this the ideal view.

Phone: +226 25 36 52 22

Trip type: Business

Travel group: Friends

Rooms: 4

Service: 4

Location: 4

Hotel highlights: Luxury, Quiet, Kid-friendly, Great valueAddress: Burkina Equipements, Dassasgo, Ouagadougou, Burkina Faso

CHAPTER SEVEN

Natural Wonders and Breathtaking Landscapes

Sahara Desert and Sahel Region

The Sahara Desert, which spans North Africa, is the biggest hot desert on Earth. It's a rough area of sand dunes, rocky plateaus, and high temperatures, covering over 3.6 million square kilometers. Life has adapted to the dry climate, with hot daytime highs and freezing evenings. Its expanse is navigated by nomadic tribes like the Tuareg, and the Sahara's ergs, enormous dunes, are recognisable features.

The Sahel Region, a transitional region that stretches across Africa from the Atlantic Ocean to the Red Sea, is located next to the Sahara. It is an important ecological and agricultural zone with a semi-arid climate. The Sahel is an area with many different cultures and tenacious tribes working to adapt to its changing environment, despite problems like desertification and food poverty.

Majestic Waterfalls and Rainforests

West Africa is home to some of the continent's most magnificent waterfalls and lush jungles. The breathtaking Nimba Falls, which cascade down high cliffs in Guinea, are located there. They are encircled by a thick jungle filled with biodiversity. The breathtaking man-made wonder in Cote d'Ivoire is where a river plunges 105 meters, providing a breathtaking spectacle. These natural wonders are found in the Upper Guinean Forest, which spans multiple West African nations and provides a haven for endangered animal species like chimpanzees and bird species. A voyage into the heart of West Africa's natural beauty, these waterfalls and rainforests are a tribute to the area's ecological richness.

Exploring the Beaches of Ghana

Ghana has a coastline that is lined with interesting and alluring beaches. Busua Beach's calm coastlines, a surfer's heaven, appeal with its beautiful waves and golden sand. With its lush rainforest meeting the sea at Cape Coast, Kakum National Park offers a distinctive coastal experience. A quiet refuge for relaxation and water sports is created farther east where the Atlantic and the estuary of Ada Foah meet. Beyond that, Accra's crowded Labadi Beach offers a lively ambiance with beachfront bars and cultural events. Even though Ghana's beaches are not as well-known as some others, they are undiscovered jewels that are worth visiting since they reflect the nation's rich culture, stunning scenery, and kind people.

Senegal's Coastal Gems

On the westernmost tip of Africa, Senegal is home to a treasure trove of coastal beauties that draw tourists in with their natural beauty and historical significance. The historic Goree Island, famed for its past as a slave trading post, is located in Dakar, the energetic capital city, which is situated along the Atlantic Ocean. Visitors can explore the local museums and take in the somber memories of a terrible past.

The tranquil beaches, fishing communities, and breathtaking Pink Lake are all found along the Petite Côte, which continues down the coast further south. The lake's distinctive pink color, brought on by algae and high salt levels, creates an odd appearance. The Sine-Saloum Delta opens for nature lovers with its complex web of canals, mangroves, and varied animals. It is a UNESCO Biosphere Reserve and a birdwatcher's heaven.

The colonial architecture and diverse cultural fusion of Saint-Louis, a UNESCO World Heritage site in the north, represent the city's past as a major trading center. Sea turtles and a variety of birds are protected in the neighboring Langue de Barbarie National Park. The historical and scenic coastline beauties of Senegal make for an interesting and rewarding trip.

Watersports and Marine Life in The Gambia

The Atlantic coast of West Africa's The Gambia is home to a variety of aquatic activities and a thriving marine ecosystem. It is a paradise for enthusiasts thanks to its pleasant temperature and breathtaking shoreline. Canoeing down the tranquil River Gambia offers a tranquil experience, while thrill-seekers can kite surf the Atlantic's waves.

The Gambia's marine life is very fascinating. Its coastal waters are home to a wide variety of animals, making it a haven for those who enjoy watching birds and other wildlife. Examples of The Gambia's abundant biodiversity include the Tanbi Wetlands and Abuko Nature Reserve, which are home to crocodiles, hippos, and a wide variety of bird species. Sea turtles that are in danger of going extinct nest along the coast, particularly in places like Kartong and Sanyang.

The beautiful underwater world is revealed via snorkeling and scuba diving, and it is alive with colorful fish, coral reefs, and even the occasional dolphin or manatee sighting. In The Gambia, marine life and watersports combine to provide an amazing experience that highlights the nation's biodiversity and natural beauty.

Exploring Saharan Dunes in Niger

All who come into this dry region are captivated by the mesmerizing Saharan dunes in Niger. These recognisable sand dunes, which span the northern section of the nation, are an essential component of the Sahara Desert, the largest scorching desert in the world. The Ténéré Desert and the Erg of Bilma are home to Niger's most known sand dunes. These enormous dunes, which the unrelenting winds have molded, may soar to dizzying heights—some of them rising more than 500 feet. They produce a fantastical world of shifting dunes and golden waves that rippling in the hot sun.

Underneath their seeming hardiness, a hidden world of adapted desert plants and fauna can be found. Adventuresome tourists and lovers of the desert are invited to explore the tranquil magnificence of the Saharan dunes in Niger. The dunes transform into vibrant red and orange as the sun sets, creating an amazing sight. Exploring these huge sandscapes offers a profound connection to the Sahara's ageless beauty and harshness in addition to a visual feast. It is a location where the earth's primitive, old powers are in full force, making a lasting impression on those who are fortunate enough to see their majesty.

Eco-Tourism in Burkina Faso's Parks

All who come into this dry region are captivated by the mesmerizing Saharan dunes in Niger. These recognisable sand dunes, which span the northern section of the nation, are an essential component of the Sahara Desert, the largest scorching desert in the world. The Ténéré Desert and the Erg of Bilma are home to Niger's most known sand dunes.

These enormous dunes, which the unrelenting winds have molded, may soar to dizzying heights—some of them rising more than 500 feet. They produce a fantastical world of shifting dunes and golden waves that rippling in the hot sun. Underneath their seeming hardiness, a hidden world of adapted desert plants and fauna can be found.

Adventuresome tourists and lovers of the desert are invited to explore the tranquil magnificence of the Saharan dunes in Niger. The dunes transform into vibrant red and orange as the sun sets, creating an amazing sight. Exploring these huge sandscapes offers a profound connection to the Sahara's ageless beauty and harshness in addition to a visual feast. It is a location where the earth's primitive, old powers are in full force, making a lasting impression on those who are fortunate enough to see their majesty.

Hiking Adventures in Sierra leone

This undiscovered treasure is located in West Africa and features stunning beaches, lush jungles, and steep mountains. The climb up Mount Bintumani, the tallest mountain in West Africa other than Cameroon, is one of the most well-known hikes. The ascent to the summit promises to be difficult but rewarding, with sweeping views of the surroundings.

Hikers can visit the Tiwai Island Wildlife Sanctuary to experience a distinctive fusion of nature and history. In this deep rainforest reserve, unique primates and pygmy hippos, both of which are endangered, can be found. It is possible to get a taste of Sierra Leone's diverse biodiversity by trekking across this lush landscape. The coastal areas of Sierra Leone also appeal to adventure seekers. Savannahs and riverine woods in the Outamba-Kilimi National Park encourage hikers to explore its gorgeous landscapes and spot a variety of species.

Sierra Leone's hiking excursions promise life-changing experiences in a place where nature and culture perfectly coexist, whether you're looking for rough mountain summits, deep rainforests, or coastline vistas.

CHAPTER EIGHT

Cultural Heritage and Historical Sites

The Legendary Timbuktu

The famous city of Timbuktu, whose name has long piqued people's interest, is situated in Mali, in West Africa. Its historical importance derives from its function as a thriving hub of trade, culture, and learning during the 14th-century Mali Empire's heyday.

The strategic location of Timbuktu along trans-Saharan trade routes, which enabled the exchange of gold, salt, ivory, and other priceless commodities, was a major factor in the city's popularity. Timbuktu became a center of intellectual and cultural interchange as a result of the scholars, poets, and travelers that its affluence drew from all corners of the Islamic world. Ancient manuscripts from the city, which cover a wide range of subjects like astronomy, mathematics, medicine, and Islamic theology, are well-known.

These manuscripts offer insightful perspectives on the intellectual development of Africa and its contributions to world knowledge. The late 16th century saw the beginning of Timbuktu's collapse as trade routes changed and empires faded. However, it has left a lasting impact as a representation of African intellectualism, tenacity, and historical importance.

Timbuktu was recognised for its cultural and historical significance when UNESCO named it a World Heritage Site in 1988. Timbuktu, a fabled city that continues to capture the imagination of people all over the world, remains as a tribute to the persevering spirit of human exploration and knowledge-seeking today.

Ghana's UNESCO World Heritage Sites

Two outstanding UNESCO World Heritage Sites in Ghana showcase the country's significant cultural heritage and rich history. Elmina, Cape Coast, and Beyin Fortifications: These coastal defenses, constructed by European nations during the height of the transatlantic slave traffic, serve as a somber reminder of Ghana's participation in this ominous era of history. Key examples include Elmina Castle, Cape Coast Castle, and Fort Apollonia. They include evidence of the terrible slave trade, including the dungeons where Africans were imprisoned as slaves prior to their perilous trips. These locations stand for the Ghanaian people's tenacity and struggle for freedom.

Asante Traditional Buildings: Situated in the Ashanti area, these ancient structures represent the Asante people's rich architectural and cultural legacy. The buildings, which include palaces, shrines, and traditional houses, exhibit dexterous handiwork and beautiful detailing. They also provide as living proof of the Asante Kingdom's ongoing observance of ancient traditions and rites. These Ghanaian UNESCO World Heritage Sites offer priceless insights into the past of the nation, from its somber colonial history to its vivacious cultural traditions. In addition to being significant historical sites, they serve as vital educational tools that support the appreciation and preservation of Ghana's past for coming generations.

Benin's Kingdoms and Palaces

The historical kingdom of Benin in West Africa is home to numerous former kingships and palaces that have profoundly influenced the history and culture of the area. The Great Kingdom of Benin and the Oyo Empire are principally linked to the history of the kingdom. The Great Kingdom of Benin, which arose in the 13th century, was famed for its highly developed government, stunning artwork, and potent military. Its impressive mud walls, some of which were as long as 16,000 kilometers, encircled the capital of the kingdom, Benin City, during their height in the 15th and 16th centuries.

These walls acted as both protective fortifications and representations of the kingdom's might and power. The Oba's Palace, the center of the kingdom, served as a symbol of Benin's accomplishments in terms of culture and the arts inside the city. The palace was adorned with elaborate bronze statues and plaques that demonstrated the kingdom's ability of metalworking and craftsmanship. These artifacts, which portray historical occurrences and court life, are now renowned across the world for their artistic value.

A big part of Benin's history was also played by the Oyo Empire, a nearby superpower. The city of Oyo-Ile, with its stunning architecture and organized social order, became the Great Kingdom's political and cultural center after its influence caused the Great Kingdom to fall. The ruins of these kingdoms and palaces still enthrall historians, archaeologists, and tourists today by providing a glimpse into Benin's rich history and its long-lasting cultural influence.

Slave Trade Routes and Heritage Sites

Slave Trade Routes and Heritage Sites in West Africa commemorate the people's tenacity while bearing testimony to a sombre period in human history.

Millions of Africans were forcibly removed from their homes between the 16th to 19th centuries as a result of the transatlantic slave trade and sent to the Americas and Europe. The capture and transportation of slaves was made easier by the intricate network of highways, rivers, and ports that made up the West African slave trade routes. Goree Island in Senegal, Cape Coast Castle in Ghana, and Elmina Castle in Nigeria were important hubs where numerous men, women, and children were imprisoned in appalling conditions before their agonizing passage across the Atlantic. These locations serve as sombre reminders of the crimes done during the era of the slave trade today. They are revered as UNESCO World Heritage Sites and stand as a testament to recollection and peace.

Visitors can contemplate the atrocities of the past as they tour the dungeons, shackles, and tight cells were enslaved Africans faced unfathomable misery. As visitors to these cultural sites see the tenacity of African civilizations that have endured for millennia in the face of adversity, they are also inspired by a profound sense of unity and resiliency. They provide a forum for discussion and education, making sure that the world never forgets the lasting effects of the transatlantic slave trade on West Africa.

Ancient Kingdoms and Archaeological

West Africa's significant historical past. Of these, the Kingdom of Ghana, which dates to the fourth century, signaled the beginning of the area's development as a hub for trade and culture. It flourished thanks to trade routes that crossed the Sahara Desert and was well-known for its gold deposits. Following Ghana, the Mali Empire rose to power under Mansa Musa in the 14th century. His well-known journey to Mecca served as a display of Mali's enormous wealth, establishing its international fame. Mali's Timbuktu developed into a renowned center of study that has preserved innumerable manuscripts and old documents.

Between the 14th to the 17th centuries, Benin, another West African state, prospered. The superb Benin Bronzes, which are now sought-after archaeological treasures in museums all over the world, were among its famed works of skilled art. It is well known for its superb bronze and terra-cotta sculptures that date back more than a thousand years, which are found in the Kingdom of Ife in what is now Nigeria. These works of art provide a window into the advanced metallurgy and artistic expertise of the area.

Archaeologists are still finding these riches today, providing light on the storied past of West Africa. These ancient kingdoms and their archaeological treasures highlight the region's historical significance and cultural legacies, encouraging academics and history buffs to learn more about this fascinating past.

CHAPTER NINE

Arts, Music, and Festivals

West African Music and Rhythms

A huge region of the African continent, including nations like Nigeria, Senegal, Mali, Ghana, and many others, is home to the rich and diverse musical legacy known as West African music. The intricate rhythms, bright melodies, and profound cultural significance of West African music distinguish it from other genres.

Rhythms: The intricate and polyrhythmic patterns seen in West African music are well known. Layers of rhythmic textures are produced by using a variety of percussion instruments, including djembe drums, talking drums, congas, and balafons. The appeal of the music is mostly due to the way these rhythms are frequently weaved together, creating a mesmerizing and hypnotic effect.

Instruments: There are several different native instruments in the area, each with a distinctive sound. The harp-like instrument known as the kora is a mainstay of Senegalese and Gambian music. In Mali and Guinea, the balafon, a xylophone-like instrument, is frequently heard. Speaking drums, like the Dundun in Nigeria, are used to convey messages and imitate speech.

Melodies: Vocals and stringed instruments like the kora and ngoni frequently feature in West African music. Vocal harmonies are typical, and performers frequently engage in call-and-response interactions with listeners or other performers. The region's musical tradition is transmitted and preserved by griots, or oral historians, through song-based narrative.

Dance and rites: In West Africa, religious and cultural rites have a close connection to music. Music and rhythm are essential components of all rituals, whether they be spiritual rites or traditional dances to celebrate harvests. These celebrations frequently feature intricate dancing, colorful costumes, and masks.

West African music has had a significant influence on international music genres. Jazz, blues, reggae, and even modern pop music have all been affected by the rhythms and instruments. Popular performers like Fela Kuti and Miriam Makeba introduced West African music to a global audience.

Modern Fusion: Incorporating modern elements like electronic beats and Western instruments, contemporary West African musicians have embraced fusion in a variety of musical genres. As a result of this combination, new genres including Afrobeat and Afro-pop were developed.

Regional Variation: Due to West Africa's size, its music differs significantly from one subregion to another. For example, the high-energy, guitar-driven music of Mali contrasts with the Afrobeat of Nigeria, famed for its brass parts and socially aware lyrics.

Griot tradition as it is practiced today: West African music and culture are fundamentally based on the Griot tradition. Oral historians and storytellers known as griots transmit history, morals, and wisdom to future generations through song. They are well-respected members of their communities and frequently perform with instruments like the kora or balafon.

Mbalax, or Senegal's Groove, is a distinct musical style made popular by performers like Youssou N'Dour. Mbalax is known for its contagious rhythms, which combine conventional Sabar drumming with more contemporary instruments like electric guitars and synthesizers. It drives Senegal's thriving nightlife and festivities.

Nigeria's Contributions to Highlife and Afrobeat West African music has benefited greatly from Nigeria. Afrobeat was inspired by the blend of African rhythms and Western jazz found in highlife. Jazz, funk, and Yoruba musical influences are all combined to create the danceable rhythms and political lyrics of afrobeat, which

166

was invented by Fela Kuti. West African musicians frequently don colorful, ornate clothes, such as the renowned Kente cloth from Ghana, which is also known as a type of cloth. These clothes often carry messages, stories, or social standing in addition to being aesthetically pleasing. The clothing gives the music and performances a new visual dimension.

Music for Spiritual and Healing Practises: West African music is widely used in spiritual and therapeutic procedures. Certain rhythms and songs are believed to have therapeutic properties, and they are used in rituals to connect with the divine, heal the sick, or guide individuals through life transitions.

Modern Global Stars: West African musicians have achieved global stardom in recent years. Artists like Burna Boy and Wizkid from Nigeria and Amadou & Mariam from Mali have garnered international acclaim, blending traditional sounds with contemporary music genres.

Dance and Movement: West African music is inseparable from dance. Dancers often interpret the rhythms with intricate footwork and body movements. Dance is not just a form of entertainment but also a means of social expression and communication.

Community and Celebration: Music in West Africa is communal. It brings people together for various celebrations, including weddings, funerals, religious ceremonies, and festivals. These events serve as a way for communities to bond and express their shared identity.

Influence on Other Arts: West African music extends its influence beyond the auditory domain. It has inspired various forms of art, including visual arts, literature, and even fashion. The vibrant patterns and colors seen in West African textiles and art are reflected in the music's lively spirit.

West African music and rhythms are a treasure trove of cultural richness, history, and artistic expression. They continue to evolve while maintaining their deep-rooted traditions, ensuring that this musical heritage remains a vibrant force in the global cultural landscape.

Traditional Dance and Performance Arts

When it comes to traditional dance and performance arts, West Africa is a rich and diverse continent. These artistic disciplines are firmly ingrained in the cultures of the many West African countries and serve a variety of functions, from celebrating happy occasions to telling tales and passing down cultural traditions, to conveying a wide range of messages. Here is a summary of some important elements of traditional dance and performance in West Africa:

Diversity of Cultures: There are many different ethnic groups in West Africa, each of which has its own distinctive dances and performance customs.

These groups, which individually add to the rich tapestry of West African dance, include the Yoruba, Igbo, Hausa, Fulani, Mandinka, Ashanti, and many others.

Ritual and Symbolism: Traditional West African dancing frequently assumes a prominent position in social and religious rites. Dancers don elaborate masks and costumes, and their motions can include rich symbolism. For instance, the Yoruba "Gelede" dance is a mask dance that honors and appeases ancestral spirits, and the Krobo "Dipo" dance of Ghana celebrates the maturation of girls into women.

Live Drumming: Drums and other percussion instruments are a crucial component of West African dancing. The drums' beats convey messages and feelings in addition to giving dancers a beat. Drummers are incredibly revered and important to the performance.

The art of narrating stories through dance is prevalent in West African music and dance. They relate myths, stories, and historical occurrences.

For instance, the Guere people of the Ivory Coast perform the "Kakilambe" dance, which uses complex dance steps to tell the tale of a mythological hero. elaborate costumes and masks are frequently used in West African dance. These include elaborate motifs and vivid colors and are frequently handmade. The masks give a spiritual element to the play because they represent spirits and ancestors rather than just being decorative. West African dancing is sometimes a collective endeavor that involves the entire village or community. It serves to celebrate significant anniversaries in community members' lives and promotes a sense of cohesion and unity.

Influence on Contemporary Dance: The world's contemporary dance genres have been greatly influenced by West African dance. Hip-hop and modern dance, among other dance genres, also incorporate aspects of West African dance, such as syncopation and polyrhythmic motions.

Celebrations and Festivals: Traditional dance and performance arts are celebrated and honored in many West African nations. These events draw both locals and visitors and serve to highlight the area's rich cultural heritage. Finally the traditional dance and performance arts of West Africa are steeped in tradition, spirituality, and narrative. In addition to providing entertainment and a reason to celebrate, they help keep and pass along traditions. These artistic disciplines continue to flourish and stimulate innovation both locally and internationally.

Festivals Celebrating Spirituality and Culture

The spirituality and cultural diversity of West Africa is reflected in the vivid celebrations that make up its festivals. Here are a few West African festivals that honor spirituality and culture:

Festival of the Niger (Mali): This yearly celebration of the Niger River, a source of life for many West African people, takes place in Ségou, Mali.

It highlights the mystical bond between the people and the river through traditional music, dance, and art displays.

Nigeria's Osun-Osogbo Festival is a Yoruba celebration that takes place in the grove of the goddess of fertility and water, Osun. People assemble to worship Osun and ask for her blessings on their well-being and wealth. It mixes artistic performances, vibrant processions, and drumming.

Panafest (Ghana): The Pan-African Historical Theatre Festival brings together Africans from all over the world to celebrate their common heritage. It is held every two years in Cape Coast, Ghana. It includes discourses on African spirituality and cultural identity in addition to music, dance, and theater.

Vodun Festival (Benin): Vodun, which is frequently erroneously referred to as "voodoo," is a major religion in Benin. In Ouidah, the yearly Vodun Festival honors ancestors' spirits and gods.

It includes intricate rituals carried out by priests and followers, as well as ceremonies and trance dances.

The Durbar Festival is a celebration of traditional horsemanship, martial arts, and cultural exhibits that takes place throughout northern Nigeria. It is a major cultural and spiritual occasion since it frequently involves prayers and spiritual rites.

Homowo Festival (Ghana): To commemorate the end of a time of famine, the Ga people of Accra, Ghana, celebrate the Homowo Festival. After performing rituals to placate the spirits, people dance and eat traditional foods like "kpoi kpoi."

Event au Desert (Mali): This music event in the Sahara Desert of Mali brings together Tuareg and other ethnic groups, despite difficulties it has faced recently due to security concerns. The chance to honor their nomadic lifestyle via song, dance, and storytelling is presented.

Eyo Festival (Nigeria): Eyo is a cultural festival held in Lagos, Nigeria. It is often referred to as the "Adamu Orisha Play" and is dedicated to the Yoruba deity, Eyo. Participants, adorned in white robes and colorful hats, parade through the streets, and the festival combines elements of masquerade, music, and spirituality.

Igue celebration (Nigeria): This royal celebration honors the Oba (king) and is observed by the Edo people of Nigeria. It entails a number of rites that are thought to reinforce the community's spiritual and cultural bonds, such as honoring the ancestral shrines of the kingdom.

Festival of Masks (Ivory Coast): In Ivory Coast, numerous ethnic groups celebrate with colorful masks, such as the Guro Goli masks or the Yoruba Gelede masks. These masks are not just artistic expressions but also have spiritual significance, often representing deities, ancestors, or mythological figures.

FESPACO - Pan-African Film and Television Festival of Ouagadougou (Burkina Faso): **FESPACO** is one of Africa's most prestigious film festivals. Despite having a strong film component, it also acts as a cultural forum for exploring and debating spirituality, identity, and societal concerns through the eyes of African filmmakers.

Abeokuta Festival (Nigeria): Abeokuta, a city in southwestern Nigeria, hosts an annual cultural festival that includes music, dance, and colorful processions. It celebrates the heritage of the Egba people and their history, including their resistance to colonialism.

Dipo Festival (Ghana): Among the Krobo people of Ghana, the Dipo Festival is a rite of passage for young girls entering womanhood. It includes spiritual ceremonies, traditional dances, and the donning of beaded attire. The festival emphasizes cultural values and female empowerment.

Ngondo Festival (Cameroon): The Ngondo Festival, held by the Duala people in Douala, Cameroon, celebrates the sea and its importance in their culture. It includes rituals, regattas, and the election of the "King of Waters" to honor their spiritual connection to the ocean.

These festivals are essential components of West African culture, blending spirituality, art, and community to preserve and celebrate the rich heritage of the region. They provide a window into the diverse belief systems, traditions, and artistic expressions that define West Africa's cultural landscape.

Adventure and Outdoor Activities

West Africa provides a wide variety of outdoor activities and adventure tours. This area contains a variety of landscapes, from lush rainforests to dry deserts. Here are a few thrilling pursuits you can partake in in West Africa:

Safari Adventures: Take a safari to discover West Africa's diverse wildlife. Elephants, lions, and antelopes can all be seen in their native environments in nations like Senegal, Mali, and Burkina Faso.

Gorilla Trekking: You can embark on gorilla trekking trips in nations like Sierra Leone, Liberia, and Guinea. It's a rare and unforgettable experience to track these majestic animals through the impenetrable woodlands.

Desert excursions: The enormous desert landscapes of Mauritania and Niger are well-known. Experience the bizarre beauty of the Sahara Desert, replete with towering sand dunes and starry evenings, by going on camel treks.

Water Sports: The Atlantic Ocean coast of West Africa offers numerous options for participating in water sports. Kiteboarding in Ghana, surfing in Cape Verde, or simply unwinding on a gorgeous beach are all options.

Trekking and hiking: There are many mountains and hills in West Africa. Hikers can travel over the hills of Togo, the verdant Fouta Djallon highlands in Guinea, or Mount Cameroon.

Cultural exploration: West Africa has a diverse cultural past in addition to its natural splendor. Visit rural villages or explore historic places like Timbuktu in Mali to get a sense of the local traditions, music, and dance.

Canoe safaris: You may go on canoe safaris through luxuriant mangrove forests in nations like Ghana and Benin, providing a distinctive viewpoint on the area's different ecosystems and fauna.

Rock Climbing: Ghana, Mali, and Burkina Faso provide chances for novice and expert climbers to engage in rock climbing. The terrain is difficult due to the rocky outcroppings and landforms.

White-Water Rafting: For thrill-seekers, white-water rafting on the Volta River in Ghana or the Niger River in Guinea provides a thrilling experience with difficult rapids and breathtaking landscapes.

Fishing excursions are great in the rivers and coastal regions of West Africa. Join fishing expeditions to catch barracuda, tuna, and snapper, among other fish species.

Caving: Venture into the limestone caves of West Africa to see its hidden beauties. For instance, Burkina Faso is well-known for its interesting cave systems, such as the Domes de Fabedougou.

Bike Tours: Take a bike trip to explore the area on two wheels. Cycling paths are available in Senegal and Ghana that pass through picturesque regions and lively local communities.

Quad bike: Quad biking through the desert is a thrilling way to explore the arid landscape in nations like Senegal and Mali.

Ecotourism: Many West African nations are dedicated to responsible travel and provide ecotours that emphasize conservation initiatives and highlight the region's distinctive flora and fauna.

Surf fishing: Go on fishing excursions along the coast with local fishermen. You can learn about local fishing customs using this time-tested, environmentally friendly method.

Hot Air Ballooning: You can go on hot air balloon trips to enjoy a bird's-eye perspective of the beautiful landscapes and quaint towns in Mali's Dogon Country and other gorgeous places.

Overland Safaris: If you want to see a range of landscapes, cultures, and adventures all in one trip, think about going on an overland safari tour that travels across many West African nations.

Stargazing: West Africa is a fantastic location for stargazing due to its vast deserts and minimal levels of light pollution. Here, the nighttime skies are frequently clear as day, providing stunning views of the stars and other celestial objects. Adventurers and outdoor enthusiasts find West Africa to be an intriguing destination due to its diverse geography and rich cultural heritage. This area offers thrilling adventures as well as serene natural beauty, so there is something for everyone to enjoy.

CHAPTER TEN

Spiritual Journeys and Sacred Sites

West Africa is home to several spiritual practices and holy places that have long been important to the different populations there. The region's cultural and religious variety, which includes influences from indigenous beliefs to Islam and Christianity, is demonstrated by these spiritual excursions and hallowed sites.

The Nigerian sacred grove of Osun-Osogbo This UNESCO World Heritage Site honors the Yoruba deity Oshun and is situated in Nigeria's southwest Osun State. The grove, a verdant woodland that encircles the Osun River, is a sacred site for Yoruba believers. Devotees from all over the world travel to the yearly Osun-Osogbo festival to honor the goddess.

Jenne-Jeno (Mali): This historical location, also known as Djenné-Djenno, is regarded as one of the continent's earliest urban centers. It has tremendous historical and spiritual significance for the people of Mali and was once a center for trade and culture. The location houses religious artifacts and old burial grounds.

Sufi Brotherhoods (Senegal and Mali): Senegal and Mali are two countries in West Africa with a rich Sufi Muslim legacy. The Mouride Brotherhood built the Senegalese city of Touba, which is a popular destination for Sufi Muslims to travel to. Timbuktu, a town in Mali, has long served as a hub for Sufi education and spiritual inquiry.

Ifa is a form of divination that links people with the spirit world, and it is practiced by the Yoruba people of Nigeria and Benin. The Nigerian city of Ile-Ife is revered as the spiritual center of Ifa, and practitioners frequently travel there to consult with priests and establish contact with their ancestors.

The Stone Circles of Senegambia (Senegal and The Gambia) are thought to have had spiritual and ritual importance and date from between the third century BC and the sixteenth century AD. They are widespread throughout Senegal and The Gambia, and scholars continue to study and admire their function and cultural significance.

Elmina Castle (Ghana): Elmina Castle has a somber past as a slave trafficking center, but it also has spiritual value for many people. For individuals desiring to pay tribute to the memories of their ancestors who suffered there during the transatlantic slave trade, it has served as a place of pilgrimage and reflection.

Mali is the home of the Dogon people, who practice a distinctive spirituality and cosmology. In order to maintain harmony with the spirit world and ancestors, the Dogon hold rites and ceremonies at a number of sacred locations on the Bandiagara Escarpment, including caves and cliffs.

These holy places and pilgrimages in West Africa are evidence of the rich and varied civilizations of the continent. They act as centers for introspection, worship, and cultural preservation, preserving for future generations the spiritual practices and past that make up this diverse region of the world.

Voodoo Traditions in Benin

In Benin, West Africa, voodoo, also known as "Vodou or Voodoo, is a well-known and intricate religious and cultural institution. An outline of Voodoo customs in Benin is shown below:

Voodoo originated in West Africa and was transported to the Americas during the transatlantic slave trade. It combines native Caribbean and Latin American traditions with aspects of Christianity and native African beliefs. Voodoo practitioners engage with a pantheon of spirits (loas) that serve as the intermediaries between people and the divine and believe in a supreme god named Mawu-Lisa.

Voodoo ceremonies frequently take place at temples or shrines as places of worship and ritual. They include dancing, making sacrifices to the spirits, and music. Possession, in which participants are said to be taken over by a loa and given guidance and healing, is one type of ritual. In other rites, animal sacrifices are also frequent.

Ancestor Worship: In voodoo, ancestors are revered greatly. Practitioners honor their ancestors in order to receive protection and direction from them. In both homes and communities, ancestor altars are prevalent.

Voodoo is well-known for its healing techniques and divination techniques. Voodoo priests and priestesses, also referred to as "houngans" and "mambos," treat physical and spiritual ills using plants, charms, and ceremonies. To predict the future, divination techniques including shell throwing and object pattern analysis are used.

Community and Social Structure: Benin's social structure is significantly influenced by voodoo. It helps build a sense of community, and practitioners frequently meet together for celebrations of their common traditions during festivals and rituals.

Festivals: The annual Fête du Vodoun, held on 10 January every year, is the most well-known voodoo celebration in Benin. It draws tourists from all over the world and exhibits lively rituals, music, dance, and ceremonies.

Misconceptions: Because of how voodoo is portrayed in popular culture, it is frequently misunderstood and stigmatized. Actually, it is a richly varied and profoundly spiritual tradition that many Beninese people strongly associate with their cultural identity.

Voodoo received recognition from UNESCO in 2008 as an Intangible Cultural Heritage of Humanity, recognising its importance to culture and the need to conserve its traditions. Benin has a rich and diverse voodoo culture that reflects both the people's continuing spiritual beliefs and the country's multiculturalism. It keeps changing and adapting while upholding its fundamental spiritual ideals.

Islamic Heritage in Mauritania

The history, culture, and society of the West African nation of Mauritania have all been significantly influenced by its rich Islamic legacy. Here are some significant facets of Mauritania's Islamic heritage:

Early Islamic Influence: Arab traders and Berber nomads brought Islam to the area in the eighth century. It gradually embedded itself profoundly into Mauritanian culture.

Islamic Republic of Mauritania: In 1958, Mauritania formally made Islam its official state religion. The identity and legal structure of the country were significantly impacted by this choice.

Maliki School of Islamic Jurisprudence: Mauritania mainly adheres to the Maliki school of Islamic law, which has an impact on its legal and spiritual practices. Sharia, or Islamic law, is a major component of the legal system in this nation.

Islamic Architecture: The cities and towns of Mauritania are clearly characterized by traditional Islamic architecture. Islamic institutions, mosques, and minarets all have elaborate designs that are frequently made of adobe.

Islamic Education: There are numerous Quranic schools () and religious scholars who instruct in Islamic theology, law, and spirituality throughout the nation.

Sufism: In Mauritania, there is a sizable presence of sufism, a mystic and spiritual branch of Islam. Particularly powerful and well-respected are the Tijaniyya and Qadiriyya Sufi organizations.

Nomadic herders in Mauritania have kept their Islamic tradition alive despite living in far-off desert areas. These nomadic groups continue to follow distinctive Islamic customs.

Islamic Holidays: In Mauritania, religious holidays like Eid al-Fitr and Eid al-Adha are widely observed. Communities get together during these times for prayers, feasts, and charity endeavors.

Islamic Art and Calligraphy: Mauritanian culture is strongly influenced by Islamic art and calligraphy. Arabic calligraphy is frequently used to decorate structures and sacred texts, highlighting the artistic side of Islamic tradition.

Islamic Values: Mauritanian society is firmly rooted in Islamic principles like hospitality, compassion, and group cohesion. These principles are demonstrated by customs like the Bayt al-Mal (community fund).

Language: Arabic is widely used in religious and educational contexts and is the official language of Mauritania. Arabic is a common language for sermons and religious writings.

Islamic Music: Islamic traditions are frequently reflected in the themes and rhythms of traditional Mauritanian music. Islamic music frequently employs instruments like the oud and .

It's crucial to remember that, despite the fact that Islam is vital to Mauritanian culture, the nation is diverse, with many different ethnic groups and traditions. This variety enhances Mauritania's Islamic heritage and adds to the country's distinctive cultural fabric.

Christianity and Animism: Togo's Spiritual Blend

Togo, a country in West Africa renowned for its cultural variety, is a special mash-up of religious beliefs and practices. Within Togo's borders, two prominent spiritual traditions coexist, showing the interesting fusion of Christianity and Animism.

Animism: Animism has a long history in Togo and is frequently practiced along with other religions.

The idea that certain natural objects—like trees, rivers, and animals—possess spirits or gods. They are adored and consulted for protection and wisdom. An important component of Togo's animism is ancestral worship, where it is believed that departed family members still affect and are present in the lives of the living.

Christianity: Over the years, Christianity, mostly in its Catholic and Protestant variants, has grown significantly in popularity in Togo. Christianity, which was introduced by European colonists during the colonial era, has distinctively melded with indigenous beliefs. A syncretic blending of cultures is the result of many Togolese Christians continuing to practice some aspects of animism alongside their Christian religion.

Syncretism: The blending of several religious practices into a unified belief system, is what gives Togo its distinctive spiritual fusion. It means that Togolese Christians frequently combine animistic rites and ideas into their worship in this environment. Those who believe in the coexistence of spiritual powers from both faiths, for instance, would seek blessings from both Christian clergy and traditional healers.

The syncretic spirituality of Togo is visible in its rituals and celebrations. Events like the "Voodoo Festival" demonstrate how animistic and Christian aspects can coexist. Visitors to sacred forests take part in rituals that include sacrifices to both animistic and Christian saints.

Challenges and Harmony: While this spiritual blending has produced a complex tapestry of practises and beliefs, it has also caused conflict between Togo's syncretists and purists of various religions. While some contend that animistic components should not be a part of authentic Christian devotion, others find peace in living lives that incorporate both faiths. In summary, the spiritual landscape of Togo is an intriguing synthesis of Christianity and Animism. This syncretism illustrates the Togolese people's ability to adapt and persevere in the face of historical and cultural changes, resulting in a distinctive and vibrant tapestry of spiritual practices that continue to shape the identity of the country.

Ancient Healing Practices and Traditional Medicine

West Africa has a long history of traditional medicine and ancient healing techniques that dates back thousands of years. These practices still play a key role in healthcare today and are firmly ingrained in the region's cultural and spiritual beliefs. In West Africa, traditional medicine has the following important components:

Herbal Treatments: In West Africa, herbal medicine is a fundamental component of traditional medicine. Practitioners, often known as herbalists or traditional healers, have a thorough understanding of the therapeutic benefits of various plants. They cure a wide spectrum of disorders with herbs, from simple illnesses to more complicated problems.

Traditional African medical practices are closely related to spiritual beliefs in West Africa. Healers frequently seek advice and healing energy from ghosts or ancestors. The healing process may include rituals, prayers, and sacrifices to appease spirits and enlist their assistance.

Divination: In order to diagnose ailments and choose the best course of treatment, divination techniques are used, such as the usage of cowrie shells, bones, or other things. For their capacity to interact with the spiritual world, diviners are held in the highest regard.

Massage and manipulation are examples of physical therapies that are used to treat a variety of physical disorders, along with bone-setting and scarification. Within particular ethnic groups, these customs are frequently passed down from generation to generation.

Diet and nutrition: Traditional healers frequently stress the need of a healthy diet in preserving wellbeing. To aid the body in healing itself, they could recommend particular foods or dietary restrictions.

Cultural diversity: The many ethnic groups that make up West Africa each have their own distinctive traditions and modes of healing. These customs might differ significantly from one area or society to another.

While traditional medicine is still crucial in West Africa, it is facing challenges as a result of the growing impact of Western medicine. To deliver more comprehensive healthcare services, efforts are being undertaken to merge traditional and modern healthcare systems.

Recognition and Regulation: A few West African nations have taken action to recognise and govern practitioners of traditional medicine. To guarantee the security and effectiveness of conventional therapies, this includes training and certification programmes. In conclusion, traditional healing methods are profoundly rooted in the spirituality and culture of West Africa. Along with contemporary medicine, they still offer healthcare options to numerous communities.

The Most Top Attractions Need To Explore

1. Kakum National Park, Ghana

Kakum National Park is situated close to the coast in Ghana's southern central region. The park was established in 1931 and designated as a national park in 1992. It was originally intended to conserve the region's diverse wildlife, including forest elephants, bongos, and numerous bird species. The total area of the national park is 145 square miles, The Kakum River, which starts inside the park, is the source of the park's name. This is the most popular natural attraction in Ghana.

Tropical forests make over 90% of the park's landscape, making them its most noticeable feature. The park's elevation ranges from 443 feet (135 meters) to 820 feet

(250 meters), and the majority of the forested area is made up of damp evergreen. There are swamp forests, riverine forests, and boval vegetation.

Buffalo, forest elephants, civets, Colobus monkeys, huge forest hogs, red river hogs, pangolins, dwarf crocodiles, and North Africa crested porcupines are among the wildlife. With the canopy walkway up in the treetops. The lofty canopy route offers a bird's-eye view and a greater chance to spot some of the creatures.

Location: Central Region of Ghana, approximately 30 km (18.6 miles) north of Cape Coast.

Coordinates: 5°21′13″N 1°23′0″W

Area: 375 km2 (145 sq mi)

Established: 1992

Hours of Operation: Open daily from 6:00 AM to 4:00 PM.

Admission: Around 60 GHS (approximately $5 USD) for adults, with additional fees for guided tours.

Average Total Time Spent: 3–5 hours.

Why You Should Visit

- Kakum National Park is ideal for adventure seekers and nature enthusiasts. Walking above the canopy gives you a close view of unique flora and fauna that are rare to find in other African parks. Bird watchers can find over 250 species, and the lush environment offers a tranquil escape.

Photography Tips

- The canopy walkway is a popular photography spot; early mornings often give the best lighting.
- Bring a zoom lens for wildlife shots and a wide-angle for landscape photos.
- Capture shots from the ground level for perspective before heading up to the walkway.

Interesting Facts

- The canopy walkway is one of only a few in Africa.
- The park is home to seven primate species and several species of large mammals.

- Local communities play a role in the park's upkeep, creating sustainable tourism.

2. Djenne, Mali

Djenné is a historic trading city in southern Mali that is also a hub for Muslim scholarship. Located 220 miles (354 km) southwest of Timbuktu, it is situated on the Bani River and on floodlands that lie between the Bani and Niger rivers. The city, which is situated on toguère, or little hills, turns into an island when the region floods seasonally. It is close to the location of Djenné-Jeno, one of the oldest towns in sub-Saharan Africa, which started to decline around the time Djenné was founded and dates back to 250 bce.

Djenné became an entrepôt between the traders of Guinea's tropical forests and those of central and western Sudan. Before being taken by Songhai emperor Sonni ʿAlī in 1468 (or 1473), the town was probably governed by the Mali empire starting in the 13th or 14th century. The city prospered by being at the forefront of the trade routes to the gold mines of Bitou (now in Côte d'Ivoire),

Lobé, and Bouré, as well as from having a direct river connection to Timbuktu. Additionally, it served as a crucial entrepôt for salt. The town was ruled by Morocco after Moroccan armies overthrew the Songhai dynasty in the sixteenth century.

Location: Djenne is located in central Mali, about 575 km (357 miles) northeast of Bamako.

Hours of Operation: The town itself is open year-round, but the Great Mosque is open to visitors only on specific days (usually Mondays).

Admission: Approximately 10,000 CFA (about $16 USD) for a guided tour of the Great Mosque.

Average Total Time Spent: 2–3 hours for a day visit, but staying overnight provides a better experience.

Why You Should Visit

- Djenne's cultural atmosphere, ancient architecture, and vibrant weekly market (Mondays) offer a unique glimpse into Mali's heritage. It's a must-see for those interested in West African history and architecture.

Photography Tips

- For the best shots of the mosque, try early morning or sunset.
- Capture the texture of the mud-brick walls close-up for unique architectural shots.
- The Monday market is a colorful, lively place perfect for street photography.

Interesting Facts

- The Great Mosque requires annual maintenance, during which the local community participates in re-coating it with mud.
- Djenne's unique mud construction is due to the semi-arid climate, which has preserved its buildings for centuries.

3. Gorée Island, Senegal

Gorée is a small, car-free island in Senegal that is located off the coast of Dakar. It is well-known for its involvement in the Atlantic slave trade from the 15th to the 19th centuries. The House of Slaves, which is now a museum, is one of the colonial structures on the winding lanes. The IFAN Historical Museum, which features displays about Senegal's past, is located in the 19th-century Fort d'Estrées. Opposite Dakar, off the coast of Senegal, is the island of Gorée. It was the biggest slave-trading hub on the African coast from the fifteenth to the nineteenth centuries. Its architecture, which was ruled successively by the Portuguese, Dutch, English, and French, is distinguished by the contrast between the gloomy slave quarters and the sophisticated homes of the slave dealers. It still acts as a haven for peacemaking and a reminder of human exploitation today.

Getting There

Île de Gorée is frequently visited and easy to get to from Dakar. A ferry runs every one or two hours from the gare maritime (passenger port) in Dakar to Gorée and is about a 25 minute boat ride. The first ferry leaves Dakar at 7am and the last ferry leaves Gorée returning back to Dakar at midnight (after 1am on Saturdays).

Estimated Cost

Bus or Taxi to Ferry Building in downtown Dakar: 150- 1.500 f cfa (Cost will depend on your location, try to bargain for a non toubab price!)

Round Trip ferry ticket:
5. 200 f cfa for a non resident adult, 2.700 f cfa for an adult resident of Africa,1.500 f cfa for an adult resident of Senegal

Lunch, snacks and drinks: 5.000 f cfa for the day Artwork, clothing, jewelry: To be honest, this depends more on how well of a haggler you are. It will also depend on what you're buying/looking for. However, a good base amount to bring is 20.000 f cfa.

Address: It is an 18.2-hectare (45-acre) island located 2 kilometers (1.1 nmi; 1.2 mi) at sea from the main harbor of Dakar

Location: Situated off the coast of Dakar, Senegal. The island is accessible via a 20-minute ferry ride from Dakar's port.

Hours of Operation: Open daily, with ferry service running from 10:00 AM to 6:00 PM.

Admission: Approximately 5,200 CFA (about $9 USD) for round-trip ferry tickets, plus a small entry fee for certain sites like the House of Slaves (Maison des Esclaves).

Average Total Time Spent: 4–6 hours.

Why You Should Visit

- Gorée Island serves as a somber reminder of history and resilience. It is both an educational and emotional experience, where visitors can reflect on the past and appreciate Senegal's cultural heritage.

Photography Tips

- The "Door of No Return" offers poignant photos.
- Capture the colorful colonial houses around the island, which contrast with the somber sites.
- Sunrise or sunset provides beautiful lighting on the harbor and enhances the island's quiet beauty.

Interesting Facts

- The island is car-free, adding to its serene atmosphere.
- Despite its dark past, Gorée is now home to artists, with galleries and studios throughout the island.
- Nelson Mandela visited Gorée as part of his efforts to acknowledge and remember the history of slavery.

4. Cape Coast Castle, Ghana

One of the largest and best-preserved slave castles on the West African coast is Cape Coast Castle, a fortified structure located in Cape Coast, Ghana. It was first established as a Portuguese trading port in 1555 and was named Cabo Corso, or "Short Cape." The original timber structure was constructed for the Swedes in 1653, and they called it Carolusborg in honor of Charles X. Gustav, their monarch. The fort was taken over by the Danes, the Dutch, and the British starting in 1664.

Over the course of the following century and a half, the British transformed the stone fort into a much bigger and more formidable structure, complete with cannons, which gave it its current appearance by roughly 1795. The most profitable business at the time the British took control of Cape Coast was the sale of African slaves, and prisons were built beneath the fortified fortress. Up to 1,500 Africans were detained in the castle dungeons at any given time while they awaited the next slaving ship in the 18th century, when Cape Coast was one of the main ports for the transatlantic slave trade.The homes and offices that the British enjoyed within the castle walls were in stark contrast to the conditions in the dungeons. The slave trade in Ghana did not end until around 1870, despite the British outlawing it in 1807.

For a brief while beginning in 1821, Cape Coast Castle served as the capital of the British colony of the Gold Coast. However, in 1877, the British relocated their capital to Accra. The British repaired the castle in the 1920s. In 1957, Ghana gained independence, and in

1974, Cape Coast Castle was made a museum. In the early 1990s, the castle underwent additional repair.

Address: Victoria Rd, Cape Coast, Ghana

Tel : +233-3321 32529, +233 57 710 1707

Hours of Operation: Open daily from 9:00 AM to 4:30 PM.

Admission: Around 40 GHS (approximately $3.50 USD) for adults, with guided tours available for an additional fee.

Average Total Time Spent: 2–3 hours.

Coordinates: 5°06'13"N 1°14'28"W / 5.10361°N 1.24111°W

Why You Should Visit

Visiting Cape Coast Castle is a profound experience, allowing you to walk through dungeons were enslaved Africans were kept and see the "Door of No Return." It offers deep historical insight and an opportunity for reflection.

Photography Tips

- Capture the view from the castle, showing both the coast and the fortress.
- Interior shots of the dungeons can convey the scale and intensity of the site's history.
- Wide shots of the entire castle structure, especially at sunrise or sunset, highlight its imposing architecture.

Interesting Facts

- Cape Coast Castle has been visited by high-profile figures, including Barack Obama.
- It's a UNESCO World Heritage site and part of the "Castles and Forts of Ghana" collective.
- The castle was pivotal in trade, not only for the slave trade but also for goods like gold and timber.

Each of these destinations provides an immersive journey through West African history, culture, and natural beauty. Enjoy your trip to this richly historic and diverse region.

Relaxation and Rejuvenation Spots

West Africa is an area renowned for its rich culture, varied landscapes, and an increasing emphasis on getaways for rest and renewal. Here are some of the best locations in West Africa for relaxation and rejuvenation:

Africa's northwest coast are the Cape Verde Islands, which are known for their gorgeous beaches, crystal-clear waters, and relaxed environment. The all-inclusive resorts on the islands of Sal and Boa Vista are especially well-known, making them excellent for unwinding.

Ghana's Coastline: Beautiful beaches and resorts can be found all along Ghana's coastline along the Gulf of Guinea. A wonderful fusion of relaxation, water sports, and vivacious local culture can be found in locations like Busua, Ada Foah, and Kokrobite.

Lac Rose, often known as the Pink Lake, is a special natural marvel in Senegal. The water has a pink tint because of the high salt content. It is easy for visitors to float in the lake, which is claimed to have healing effects. Lodges nearby offer a tranquil retreat from city life.

Gambia's Wellness Retreats: Known for its hospitable inhabitants, Gambia has a number of eco-lodges and wellness retreats located along its rivers and beaches. Yoga, meditation, and spa services are available in these serene surroundings.

Banc d'Arguin National Park in Mauritania: The Banc d'Arguin National Park in Mauritania is a UNESCO World Heritage Site for nature lovers. It's a tranquil location to get in touch with nature and a birdwatcher's heaven.

Grand Bassam, Ivory Coast: Grand Bassam is a beach town with a colonial-era charm that is only a short drive from Abidjan. It is a well-liked weekend getaway location due to its tranquil beaches, upscale boutique hotels, and laid-back environment.

Beaches in Sierra Leone include River Number Two Beach near Tokeh and Lumley Beach in Freetown. These beaches are both clean and frequently uncrowded. These locations are ideal for relaxing and sunbathing.

Ogbunike Caves in Nigeria offer a sense of serenity and spirituality for a distinctive relaxing experience. The cave system's exploration and swimming in its pristine waters are restorative activities.

The Venice of Africa: Ganvié, is a stilt settlement on Lake Nokoué in Benin and is frequently referred to as such. Visitors can engage with locals, enjoy the tranquil settings, and take boat cruises through the village's waterways.

Robertsport in Liberia is a seaside community well-known for its surfing prospects, making it a fantastic vacation spot for visitors seeking to unwind by catching waves and lounging on sandy beaches.

Togo's capital, Lome, is situated on a gorgeous coastline with palm-lined beaches. It's a wonderful location for beach relaxation, market exploration, and enjoying delectable West African cuisine.

The W National Park in Niger is a refuge for wildlife enthusiasts if you enjoy the outdoors. It's the perfect location for going on safari, watching birds, and relaxing amidst the untamed splendor of the African savannah.7

The Dogon Country in Mali provides a distinctive cultural experience. Visit traditional villages, trek across the majestic Bandiagara Escarpment, and get a taste of Dogon culture.

The Bijagos Archipelago's Bubaque Island in Guinea-Bissau is renowned for its tranquilly and unspoiled beaches. It's a remote location where you can genuinely unwind.

The spectacular natural landmarks in Banfora, Burkina Faso, like the Karfiguela Waterfalls, Sindou Peaks, and the Domes of Fabedougou are well-known. It is a serene location for lovers of nature.

One of the largest protected areas in West Africa is **Comoe National Park in Côte d'Ivoire.** It provides chances to go on river cruises, go on animal safaris, and enjoy the beauty of untamed landscapes.

The verdant Fouta Djallon Highlands in Guinea, which are renowned for their waterfalls, rivers, and beautiful hiking paths. For those seeking milder weather and breathtaking scenery, it is a tranquil escape.

Erin Ijesha Waterfall in Nigeria is a magnificent waterfall that is located in the state of Osun. In its crystal-clear waters, which are surrounded by lush greenery, visitors may cool off.

Sapo National Park in Liberia boasts deep rainforests, a variety of species, and clear rivers, making it a perfect destination for nature lovers seeking an off-the-grid adventure.

Yamoussoukro, the tranquil capital of the Ivory Coast, is where you may visit the enormous Basilica of Our Lady of Peace, which is encircled by lovely gardens and a pleasant environment. West Africa is a fascinating location for rest and renewal because it is an area full of undiscovered gems and different scenery. West Africa offers a variety of relaxing vacation options, including outdoor activities, cultural exploration, and quiet seaside vacations.

CHAPTER ELEVEN

Additional Resources and Contacts

West Africa is a big, widely distributed physical area with a multicultural population that is well-known for its vibrant customs, lengthy history, and economic potential. When seeking for further information and contacts regarding West Africa, keep the following in mind:

Academic institutions: Universities and research institutes typically have specialists and resources for studying West Africa. Contacting the departments of international relations or African studies is a wise place to start.

Cultural Centers: Many places throughout the world have cultural centers or institutions to promote West African culture. These places may provide useful data, events, and networking opportunities.

Consulates and Embassies: West African countries are represented abroad by consulates and embassy personnel. Information on prospects for trade, investment, and cross-cultural contacts can be obtained from these diplomatic posts.

Non-Governmental Organizations (NGOs): A large number of NGOs operate in West Africa with a focus on healthcare, education, and economic development. These organizations frequently welcome volunteers and collaborators.

Business Chambers: Research local, national, and international business associations with an emphasis on trade and business in West Africa. They can connect you with nearby businesses and business owners. Join forums, social media groups, and online communities that focus on West African topics. Through these websites, you can connect with experts and meet people who have similar interests to yours.

Local Communities: If you reside in a city with a diverse population, you may come across West African communities or cultural groupings. Participating in these groups could be a fantastic way to learn more about the area.

Books and Publications: Research books, academic journals, and publications about West Africa. Authors, academics, and journalists frequently share insightful information as well as contact information.

Governmental institutions Consult the divisions in your own country that are in charge of overseeing foreign trade and affairs. They may be connected to and have access to resources for West Africa.

Industry-specific trade associations can provide details on contacts, regulations, and trading prospects in West Africa.

If you're thinking about traveling to West Africa, check with tourist offices for details on possible destinations, cultural experiences, and safety measures.

Centers for Language and Culture: Enroll in language lessons or cultural activities that highlight the languages and traditions of West Africa. At these locations, you can run into knowledgeable instructors and enthusiasts.

Trade Promotion Organisations: Many West African countries maintain trade promotion organizations to promote trade and investment. These agencies can assist you and connect you with neighboring businesses.

Media Outlets: To stay current on events, trends, and opportunities in the region, follow West African news outlets online and in print. Contact editors and journalists for insights.

Contact the tourism boards of the West African nations for information on travel. They can provide information on local travel operators, visa requirements, and vacation spots.

International development agencies: In West Africa, there are regional offices for agencies like the World Bank and the United Nations Development Programme (UNDP). They work on numerous development initiatives and can offer helpful connections.

Language Schools: If you're interested in learning a new language, consider attending a West African language school. Learning the language of the area can open doors to stronger cultural relationships and understanding.

Diaspora Communities: There are sizable diaspora populations in other regions of the world for several West African nations. Engage with these groups to build relationships and learn more.

Music and art festivals: The music and art sectors in West Africa are well-known for their dynamism. Meet musicians, artists, and other cultural aficionados by going to festivals, exhibitions, and other events.

Investment Agencies: Get in touch with investment promotion organizations in West African nations if you're looking for commercial and investment prospects. They are able to help you through the procedure.

Environmental Organizations: There are environmental issues in West Africa, and a number of organizations focus on sustainability and conservation initiatives. Make contact with them to discuss eco-friendly programmes.

Local Chambers of Commerce: Each nation in West Africa normally has a chamber of commerce of its own. These groups can offer details on local contacts, investment prospects, and trade laws.

Social media groups and forums: Look into online communities and discussion boards devoted to West Africa. They can be an invaluable tool for meeting people who have similar interests to yours.

Keep in mind that developing connections and learning new things requires patience and perseverance. You can find the resources you need in West Africa via networking, experiencing the local culture, and showing a real interest in the area.

Tour Operators and Guides

Expertise & Local Knowledge: West African tour guides and operators are well knowledgeable about the areas in which they operate. They are knowledgeable about the geography, history, culture, and animals of the locations they work in. They are able to deliver insightful context and information on excursions thanks to their knowledge.

Cultural and historical tours: The history and culture of West Africa are rich and diverse. Visitors have the opportunity to tour historical sites like the slave forts of Ghana's Cape Coast or the ancient city of Timbuktu in Mali. Additionally, they arrange cultural events including traditional dance performances, festivals, and trips to neighborhood markets.

species & nature safaris: West Africa is home to a variety of ecosystems and species, from the lush rainforests of Ghana and Nigeria to the savannas of Senegal and Burkina Faso. Travelers can see animals like chimpanzees, elephants, and a variety of bird species in their native habitats by taking safaris and eco-tours offered by tour operators.

Adventure tourism: West Africa has chances for water sports, hiking, and trekking for adventure seekers. Expeditions are led by guides to places where tourists can test their mettle in breathtaking natural settings, such as the Sierra Leonean Rwenzori Mountains or Guinea's Fouta Djallon Plateau.

West African food is incredibly varied, savory, and rich in texture. Food tours are organized by tour companies to teach tourists to regional cuisine, street food, and traditional culinary techniques.

Cooking workshops are another option for learning how to make traditional West African dishes.

Community participation: Sustainable tourism and community participation are given top priority by many tour companies in West Africa. They work together with local communities to give visitors chances to get to know locals, support their businesses, and discover traditional ways of life.

Language and communication: Due to the wide variety of regional tongues in West Africa, tour guides frequently speak English, French, and regional dialects. Through allowing dialogue and cross-cultural interchange, this multilingual competence improves the visitor experience.

Tour operators take care of trip arrangements, making sure that lodging, transportation, and permits are in order. They also place a high priority on safety by offering advice on safety measures, visa regulations, and other crucial travel information.

Customized Itineraries: Whether you're interested in history, wildlife, culture, or a combination of activities, tour operators can design excursions to fit specific preferences. To make the most of your time in West Africa, they may design specialized itineraries for you.

Promotion of Responsive Tourism: A large number of West African tour companies are dedicated to responsible and sustainable tourism practices. They make an effort to reduce the negative effects of travel on the environment and give back to their communities.

Historical and Cultural Diversity: There are many different ethnic groups in West Africa, each of which has its own customs and history. Tour guides frequently stress this diversity by displaying numerous cultural customs, artistic expressions, and festivals so that tourists may understand the depth of the area's cultural legacy.

Assistance with Visas and Other Travel Documents: Understanding Visa Requirements and Other Travel Documents can be challenging. When securing the required visas and permissions for your trip to West Africa, tour companies frequently provide advice and assistance.

Emergency Support: Tour operators are prepared to offer assistance and support in the case of unanticipated events. Access to medical facilities, assistance with finding misplaced or stolen property, and emergency communication services are a few examples of this.

Solo Travel or Group trips: West African tour providers can suit your preference for solo travel or group trips. While solitary travelers can choose private guided tours for a more individualized experience, group tours offer companionship and shared experiences.

Pre-Trip Orientation: To help travelers get ready for their excursion, several tour companies offer pre-trip orientation workshops or materials. This could include advice about safety precautions, packing suggestions, and local customs and manners.

Local Collaborations: Tour operators frequently have connections with lodging establishments, eateries, and service providers in a given area. This enables them to provide affordable rates and guarantee that visitors enjoy a relaxing and genuine experience.

Feedback and evaluations: It's a good idea to read evaluations of tour operators and guides before making a reservation for a tour. This can give you information on prior travelers' experiences and assist you in choosing a trustworthy operator.

Post-Trip Resources: To help you cherish and remember your West African adventure, tour operators may provide resources like photo albums, travel diaries, or chances to post about it on blogs or social media.

To make sure that your experience reflects your interests and objectives, it is crucial to discuss your preferences and expectations with the tour operator while organizing your trip to West Africa. Your trip across West Africa can be a memorable exploration of its different landscapes, cultures, and histories with the appropriate direction and assistance.

Cultural Concepts and Practices

The diversified region of West Africa is well-known for its complex and varied cultural beliefs and customs. Although there are many different ethnic groups living in this huge area, each with its own traditions and customs, there are some common cultural themes that run throughout the region:

Oral Tradition: Stories, history, and knowledge are passed down through the generations in West Africa thanks to the spoken word, music, and storytelling. Griots, often referred to as praise-singers or oral historians, are essential to maintaining this custom.

Art and craftsmanship: The complex art and craftsmanship of West Africa are well-known. Pottery, textiles, beading, and woodcarving are examples of traditional crafts. Every ethnic group has unique artistic methods and styles. West African culture is fundamentally based on music and dance. There are many different types of music, including Afrobeat, Highlife, Juju, and other traditional drumming and percussion traditions. Dance is utilized for celebrations, ceremonies, and social events and is strongly related to music.

West Africa is a melting pot of religious ideologies in terms of both religion and spirituality. African native religions, Christianity, and Islam coexist. Many West Africans combine these faiths, combining divination, ancestor worship, and spirituality into daily life. West African food is tasty and varied, with rice, yams, cassava, and plantains serving as common ingredients. Jollof rice, Egusi soup, and fufu are popular foods.
Herbs and spices are essential ingredients in West African cuisine.

Clothing and textiles: The traditional attire of the many ethnic groups in West Africa differs. Expensive clothing is frequently made from vibrant textiles, including Kente cloth and Ankara designs, and frequently reflects cultural symbols and prestige.

Family and Community: In West African culture, the idea of family is essential. There are many extended families, and family relationships are highly respected. The maintenance of social ties requires regular community gatherings and celebrations.

Masks and Rituals: Masks from West Africa have important cultural and spiritual meanings. They are utilized during a variety of ceremonies, such as harvest celebrations, funerals, and initiation rites. These masks frequently depict ancestors or ghosts.

West Africa is very linguistically varied, with hundreds of different languages being spoken there. Among the most common languages are Hausa, Yoruba, Igbo, and

Wolof. Language is a crucial component of ethnic identity and multilingualism is widespread.

Gender Roles: Although they can be conventional, gender roles in West Africa are changing. Women usually have important roles in agriculture, trade, and family decision-making, despite the fact that men and women frequently have different positions in society.

Wisdom and proverbs: The cultures of West Africa are renowned for their extensive libraries of proverbs and sayings. These sayings are used to impart knowledge, moral principles, and life lessons. They are frequently mentioned in casual conversations and narratives.

Traditional Medicine: Traditional healers and herbal medicine are essential to West African society. For a variety of diseases, many individuals turn to conventional treatments, which frequently include spiritual components.

Festivals & Celebrations: Throughout the year, West Africa is the site of a wide variety of festivals and events. Rituals, music, dance, and vibrant clothing all serve to distinguish these occasions. The Eyo Festival in Nigeria and the Voodoo Festival in Benin are two such.

Statues and sculptures: In West Africa, sculpture is a well-known medium for artistic expression. In religious and cultural contexts, wooden and metal sculptures are frequently used to represent images of ancestors, deities, or mythological animals.

African Print textiles: The vivid and colorful African print textiles, such Ankara and Adire, are used for accessories and home decor in addition to garments. They are well-known all across the world and have come to represent African identity.

Football (football) is a popular sport in West Africa and transcends national boundaries. West African nations have produced players of the highest caliber who have significantly improved the international football scene.

Matriarchy: Women hold great power and influence within the family structure and decision-making processes in some West African countries. Matrilineal societies can be seen in Ghana's Akan and Ashanti cultures.

African Diaspora: The culture of West Africa has significantly influenced the African diaspora, especially in the Americas and the Caribbean. Dance styles like samba and religious practices like santera also carry over elements of West African culture. West African culture is a dynamic fusion of tradition and adaptation that reflects the complexity of the area's history, society, and culture. It keeps changing while clinging firmly to its origins, making it an intriguing and significant piece of the global cultural mosaic.

Conclusion

Traveling through West Africa is more than just a tourist experience; it's an excursion into a land rich in culture, history, and scenic beauty. I consider the fascinating tapestry of encounters that await travelers to this dynamic region of West Africa as I draw to a close this travel guide.

In West Africa, old customs and contemporary life coexist together. You will be able to see the tenacity of cultures that have endured the test of time, from the pulsating markets of Dakar to the rhythmic beats of traditional drumming in Ghana. Language, religion, and cultural diversity are examples of the complex tapestry of people that exists here. Meeting the friendly and hospitable people of West Africa is arguably one of the most significant experiences there. The genuine and friendly hospitality of the residents gives visitors a chance to engage with them on a deep and personal level. The inhabitants of West Africa are ready to share their experiences, cuisine, and contagious laughter.

Exploration in West Africa extends to the raw beauty of its landscapes as well as just cultural exchanges. The unspoiled beaches that adorn the coastlines of nations like Senegal, Ghana, and Nigeria entice both sunbathers and lovers of water sports. The vast savannas and rainforests of nations like Liberia and the Ivory Coast provide a haven for hikers and wildlife enthusiasts who have a taste for adventure.

Without sampling the region's delectable cuisine, no trip to West Africa would be complete. Every meal is a sensory adventure that represents the different influences of the area, from the spiciness of Nigeria's jollof rice to the luscious grilled fish of Senegal's seaside settlements. You can experience flavors that dance on your taste receptors and stimulate your senses by partaking in the dynamic street food culture, which is in and of itself an adventure. For those who enjoy history, West Africa is a veritable gold mine of tales just waiting to be discovered.

Both Gorée Island in Senegal and Cape Coast Castle in Ghana stand witness to the heinous transatlantic slave trade, offering as potent reminders of humanity's propensity for both cruelty and fortitude. The ancient city of Timbuktu in Mali, on the other hand, is a reminder of the artistic and intellectual prowess of West Africa's past. Even though West Africa's tourism infrastructure has improved recently, it is still a place that rewards those who are open to surprise and adventure. The region's allure frequently resides in the chance meetings, coincidental events, and the pleasure of navigating its busy streets.

Traveling in West Africa can present some difficulties, though. It is crucial to protect the environment and be aware of regional traditions. Travelers should use caution and keep themselves up to date on local safety issues. It is imperative to take health precautions including vaccines and preventative measures against diseases like malaria.

In summary, traveling through West Africa will immerse you in a world where environment, culture, and history all blend together to create a rich tapestry of encounters. It is a location where the past shapes the present and where hope for the future exists. The connections you make here will last a lifetime, and the experiences you make here will be indelible.

Take the plunge into this extraordinary territory if you are pulled there by the lively rhythms of West African music, the enthralling tales of its past, or the friendliness of its people. Accept the unfamiliar, enjoy the flavors, and allow West Africa's passion to inspire your wanderlust. In the end, you'll realize that West Africa is more than just a place to visit; it's a life-changing experience that permanently changes your heart and spirit.

Made in the USA
Monee, IL
18 March 2025

14198744R00134